WHITAKER
HOUSE

OMAYRA
FONT

A Dream Worth Pursuing

**FIND YOUR VALUE AND FULFILL
YOUR GOD-GIVEN DESIRES**

Unless otherwise indicated, all Scripture quotations are taken from the *Holy Bible, New King James Version*®. Copyright © 1982 by Thomas Nelson. Used with permission. All rights reserved. Scripture quotations marked (NIV) are taken from *The Holy Bible, New International Version*®, NIV®, copyright © 1973, 1978, 1984, 2011 by Biblica, Inc.® Used by permission. All rights reserved worldwide. Scripture quotations marked (KJV) are taken from the King James Version of the Holy Bible. Scripture quotations marked (AMP) are taken from *The Amplified Bible*, copyright © 2015 by The Lockman Foundation, La Habra, CA 90631. All rights reserved. Scripture quotations marked (CSB) are taken from the *Christian Standard Bible*. Copyright © 2017 by Holman Bible Publishers. Used by permission. *Christian Standard Bible*®, and CSB® are federally registered trademarks of Holman Bible Publishers, all rights reserved.

The forms LORD and GOD (in small caps) in Bible quotations represent the Hebrew name for God *Yahweh* (Jehovah), while *Lord* and *God* normally represent the name *Adonai*, in accordance with the Bible version used.

Italic and bold in texts and biblical quotes indicate the author's emphasis.

A Dream Worth Pursuing:
Find Your Value and Fulfill Your God-Given Desires

Omayra Font
Website: www.omayrafont.com
Instagram: @omayrafont

ISBN: 978-1-64123-760-4 • eBook ISBN: 978-1-64123-761-1
Printed in the United States of America
© 2021 by Omayra Font

Whitaker House
1030 Hunt Valley Circle • New Kensington, PA 15068

Library of Congress Control Number (Pending)

1 2 3 4 5 6 7 8 9 10 11 **ᴜᴜ** 28 27 26 25 24 23 22 21

CONTENTS

PREFACE

*T*he first time I realized the power I had to decide my future, I was a high-school senior attending a college orientation. A guidance counselor handed each of us a small blank card and instructed us to write down where we saw ourselves five years into the future. Some of the other attendees wondered aloud, "Why?" "What for?" "Do I have to decide *now?*" and "If I don't know what I want, what do I write?"

I filled out my card quickly, and this is what I wrote: "I want to start and finish my studies." Then I added, "I want to get married, have children, and have a family." The young woman sitting behind me asked me, "What did you write?" I innocently handed her my card. She scanned my response and then proceeded to make fun of me and my desire to find a husband and start a family. Another young person seated near us pointed out, in a mocking tone, "That's not what they're asking you to write. We're here so they can help us decide what we want to study in college. They don't care if you want to get married."

This exchange turned into a decisive moment in my life. To my peers, we were performing a simple fill-in-the-blank exercise. To me, however, it was an opportunity to flesh out my vision for my entire future—including both my professional aspirations and my hope of having a family. I don't know what became of the other young people who were there with me that day. I hope they managed to conceive their dreams and make them come true. For my part, what I had in my heart at that time is precisely what I experience every day.

At that time, I desired to study law. However, once I got married and moved with my husband, Otoniel, from Puerto Rico to Florida in response to the call of God on our lives, I found myself in a town without any reputable law school available. My husband supported my desire to study law, but in the absence of a suitable institution where I could study, we discussed our options and jointly decided that I would put that dream on hold. I remember telling Otoniel that as soon as a law school opened in central Florida, I would put a pause on my work in ministry to study law and figure out whether it was God's will for me to pursue a legal career.

Ironically, the year we returned to Puerto Rico, a law school opened in Orlando, Florida. What did I make of this? That practicing law was not God's plan for my life. And that was the precise reason I decided not to study law when I returned to Puerto Rico. During that process, Otoniel very respectfully gave me the space to make the decisions that would bring me peace.

The reality is that I could have studied law several hours away from where we lived. I could have chosen to delay starting a family. But the memory of that blank card I had filled out all those years before, and the young woman's taunts over my more substantial life plans, enabled me to prioritize answering the call of God and also making room for a family. And I have no regrets whatsoever.

Whenever someone asks me, "How do I know God's dream for my life?" I share my own story. Each of us has desires, longings, and plans, but they are subject to the doors that God opens or closes, and if any adjustments become necessary, we can make them, knowing that God's plans for our lives are always *"exceedingly abundantly"* better than anything we could come up with on our own. (See Ephesians 3:20.) I want to be clear that I am not advocating an attitude of inertia that sits back and waits to see what life will bring. Even when my dreams changed, I was always in control of them, with an ear keenly attuned to God's voice on the subject.

One of my biggest dreams came true in Puerto Rico. While living in Orlando, Florida, I enjoyed driving with Otoniel through housing developments filled with old homes. I was always attracted to the less-than-desirable residences—the ones lacking curb appeal and needing significant fixes. Seeing these houses allowed me to exercise my imagination, and I would tell my husband all the improvements I would make if I were to purchase them. I didn't see these houses as old and ugly; I saw them as potential projects that would allow me to do whatever I wanted. I said to Otoniel, "Someday, I want us to buy an ugly old house and renovate it completely." Saying these words gave me great excitement, for I felt sure I would have that opportunity at some point.

When we returned to Puerto Rico, we didn't have our own house for the first few years. I was having a hard time dealing with infertility, and Otoniel called me into his office one day and said, "Would you like to go buy a house today?"

I have to say that although I wanted a house of our own, and Otoniel knew it, I never pressured him for one. I have always endeavored to avoid being a "contentious" or "quarrelsome" woman, for the book of Proverbs says, *"Better to dwell in a corner of a housetop, than in a house shared with a contentious woman"* (Proverbs 21:9) and *"A quarrelsome wife is like the dripping of a leaky roof in a rainstorm; restraining her is like restraining the wind or grasping oil with the hand"* (Proverbs 27:15–16 NIV). Many women resort to being "dripping roofs" when they desire something, treating their husbands with hostility until they get what they want. Such was not the case with me. I wanted a house, but I didn't make that the main topic of my conversations with Otoniel, the end of all arguments, or the sole focus of my life.

I said yes right away, and an hour later, I had scheduled a same-day appointment with our real-estate agent. Believe me when I tell you, Otoniel became nervous when he saw me moving so quickly. When we got into the car that afternoon to meet the agent, he seemed to be getting cold feet. He immediately laid his cards on the table, telling me exactly how much we could spend—and not a penny more. I laugh when I remember just how scared he looked!

After showing us several properties, the agent took us to a residential area where we knew the houses would be out of our budget. We toured a beautiful home that was far more than we could afford, and I thank God that it didn't tug on my heart at all. As we were driving out of the neighborhood, we passed an abandoned house in utter disrepair. Otoniel turned the car, parked in front of that house, and then looked at the real estate agent. "What about this house?" he asked. The agent explained that it was not on the market. The property was in the middle of a marital dispute, and it had been repossessed, among other issues. I will never forget when Otoniel told me, "This is our house." I want to emphasize that everything else we had seen that day made this house the ugliest, the scariest, and the most horrific thing we could have imagined.

It had no doors. The windows were broken, and those that opened did not close; those that closed did not open. It had a pool full of giant black toads. The yard was a mess; the grass had grown as tall as the first-story windows. The kitchen was so filthy that I didn't dare open the cabinets. The walls had bullet holes in them. It was a total nightmare.

We ultimately bought that "nightmare" house. Throughout the process, God was clearly with us, and He gave us a tremendous testimony of His faithfulness in our finances. When our friends and family first saw the house, they couldn't understand why we'd bought it. Within several months of our purchasing the property, I became pregnant with our third daughter, Jenibelle. Fixing up the residence became our top priority because we would need the extra space to accommodate our growing family.

Just a few months after Jenibelle was born, we moved into the house—even though the renovation was not yet complete: no doors separating the rooms, no furniture, and the windows were still broken. Having no money on hand to address those issues, we moved in with only the essentials. And yet, I remained full of joy because of how long I had envisioned renovating a house. Close friends would say to Otoniel, "Pastor, don't move your wife and daughters into that horrible house," only to hear my husband explain to them how happy I was to be so close to the fulfillment of a lifelong dream. Naturally, I would have preferred that the work be finished before we moved in, but I was not about to be fazed by our financial circumstances.

Today, ten years later, we still live in that house. It's far from the horror it used to be. It may not be the most beautiful home in the universe, but to me, it's perfect. It's just what I wanted, and I've relished the chance to spend the past decade overseeing each repair and every improvement. The process has demanded patience and a frequent shifting of priorities. Still, it's brought me untold satisfaction and joy, all because I see the fulfillment of a dream God planted in my heart all those years ago.

What God has done for me in fulfilling my dreams, He will do for you. All you must do is surrender your hopes to Him and believe in yourself as you pursue the destiny He has placed in your heart. My prayer is that these pages will propel you to value yourself as never before and chase after your dreams with unparalleled passion.

THE KEY TO CONTENTMENT AND TRUE SUCCESS

*B*eing a woman in today's world poses a challenge in deciphering the conflicting messages that society sends us. We're told, "Dream big," "Think big," or "Live your dream," and in the next moment, we hear such cautions as these: "Be realistic," "Get your head out of the clouds," "Play it safe," "Avoid unnecessary risks." Often, these cautionary messages drown out our dreams, keeping us mired in place rather than stepping out in faith and chasing the desires God has planted in our hearts until those desires fade away and we forget them altogether.

I have observed thousands of women pursuing success, whether as wives, mothers, students, entrepreneurs, employees, or in another role. Some of these women make it only halfway to their goals, often leaving some aspirations behind to go after others—and paying a very high price in the process, succumbing to the emotional toll of unfulfilled dreams. Others tire out or despair and quit without ever becoming what they intended to be. Still others become so obsessed with "doing" that they forget about "being," and, in the end, they lose sight of who they are. They fight so hard to gain acceptance and to earn others' approval, never realizing that true success isn't found "out there." Success must be born within, and "being" is essential for knowing who you are so that you can be energized and equipped to go out and accomplish everything God has planned for you to do.

Living a happy, fulfilled life as a woman starts with properly valuing yourself. Only when you value yourself will it be possible for others to value, respect, and admire you. By valuing yourself, you clothe yourself in authority, poise, decisiveness, and beauty—both inward and outward—enabling you to be a light for yourself, your family, and everyone who comes in contact with you. When you value yourself, you have access to a shield of protection in situations where others' words and opinions otherwise would have hurt you and held you back. Valuing yourself means you exude an air of leadership that causes others to listen to your wisdom and follow your godly example.

LIVING A HAPPY, FULFILLED LIFE AS A WOMAN STARTS WITH PROPERLY VALUING YOURSELF.

Read this very carefully: valuing yourself is at the heart of your greatest desires because valuing yourself entails reminding yourself of who you indeed are. To value yourself is to render continuous praise to the One who created you as a masterpiece of His perfection, a woman *"fearfully and wonderfully made"* (Psalm 139:14) in His image. To value yourself is to understand that your heavenly Father does nothing wrong, nor does He create anything defective.

Over the years, countless women have asked me how I manage to devote myself to my ministry, to a husband who loves me, and to our four daughters, all the while working as an entrepreneur and a business administrator. I have always been glad to share my "secret": I value myself! Because I know my value, I have won every fight to overcome adversity, and I am tenacious in my pursuit of whatever I set out to achieve. By knowing who I am and how valuable I am, I have remained immovable in God during every battle, large or small.

My prayer for you, woman of God, is that you will come to value yourself. Every word in this book was written by me, especially for you. I will explain what it means to value yourself, how to convey to others the fact that you value yourself, and how to use that ability as the starting point to pursue your God-given dreams.

Pursuing a dream usually demands great sacrifice. But once you understand your actual value, you can commit to learning how to manage your energy, potential, and capabilities. The proper practices and disciplines will lead you to dream beyond whatever you thought possible and to see every one of your divine dreams come true. Have courage and maintain high expectations of the results you will receive by putting into practice what you read in the following pages. It's never too late to pursue a dream. You're never too old or too far gone to do great things for God. Woman, value yourself, and realize that your dream is one worth pursuing!

Don't let the wrong eyes determine your value.

It is you who must determine your value, according to a proper perspective of yourself.

Chapter 1

WHAT IS A WOMAN WORTH?

I want to tell you two stories. The first is of a disciple who went to his master and asked, "Master, what is the worth of a human being?"

His master didn't answer the question but took a diamond out of his pocket and handed it to his disciple, with these instructions: "Go to the bazaar and ask several merchants how much this diamond is worth. You can't sell it, however! Come back and tell me how much you have been offered for it."

The disciple went to the bazaar, presented the diamond to a vegetable vendor, and asked the man how much he would give for the jewel. "I could offer you up to four kilos of potatoes," the vendor replied.

The disciple then went to a cookware shop and asked the same question. The shopkeeper said, "I could give you some bronze pots and two brass buckets."

Next, the disciple went to a custom jewelry store. After examining the diamond, the store owner said, "I can offer you a necklace and a pair of steel earrings."

The disciple then went to a jeweler, who examined the diamond and replied, "I could offer you a good sum of money for this jewel."

Finally, the disciple arrived at the finest jewelry store in the bazaar. The owner was a highly reputable jeweler, and after making a thorough examination of the diamond, he said, "My friend, this diamond is priceless. Its value is truly immeasurable! No sum of money could buy it!"

When the disciple returned to his master and told him about the various offers he had received, the master said, "I don't think you need me to explain it to you, for you have probably realized that *the value of a human being depends on who is doing the appraising.*"

The following story is about a couple I will never forget. A woman named Glory left a job she'd held for fourteen years so she could stay home and care for her son. To show his appreciation for the sacrifice his wife was making, Glory's husband, Steven, wrote an analysis of the work she now spent her days doing—cleaning, shopping, cooking, doing laundry, managing the family's finances, and so forth—and assigned a monetary value to each task. He ultimately concluded that he did not have adequate financial resources to give his wife a fair economic remuneration for her work. Steven recognized the value of his wife, giving her honor and praise for her invaluable contribution to the family through daily actions—even the seemingly trivial ones—that blessed him and their son in incalculable ways.

The diamond's value, Glory's value, and your value all depend on who is doing the appraising. Glory is fortunate to have a husband who perceives and appreciates her value. What we don't know is the value Glory places on herself. As far as the diamond goes, a lack of information and expertise prevented most vendors from perceiving the truly priceless value of that particular gemstone. Unfortunately, not all women have the blessing of listening to the right appraiser, and thus the wrong people rate their worth and determine their value. Don't let the wrong eyes determine your value. It is you who must determine your value, according to a proper perspective of yourself.

ESCAPING THE COMMODIFICATION OF INDIVIDUALS

Unfortunately, we live in a world where, in many cases, we are assigned a monetary value. We see this truth in many aspects of society. Consider this: individual states provide price lists designating compensation for damages incurred in occupational accidents. These damages are assigned a corresponding estimate of weeks of work missed. An employer must pay the injured party the designated amount, depending on the particular body part affected. For example, in the State of Connecticut, an injured hand would earn you 168 or 155 weeks' worth of compensation; a complete arm injury would earn you 208 weeks of pay if it is the dominant arm and 194 if it's the nondominant arm.[1]

The list goes to the extreme of assigning value in weeks of compensation for injured ovaries and testicles. As for the monetary value assigned to these parts, I have no comment other than to say that it gives me great satisfaction to see that the private

---

1. State of Connecticut Workers' Compensation Commission, Sec. 31-308. Workers' Compensation Act as amended to January 1, 2011. Compensation for partial incapacity, https://wcc.state.ct.us/law/wc-act/2011/31-308.htm.

parts of men and women are priced the same. It's a rare example of gender equality in monetary issues, with women generally earning less than men and the female species being subject to bride-prices and the practice of dowry payments in many countries still today.

But is this the way to quantify the value of a person—by calculating the total worth of our body parts or the cost of producing replacement parts in a laboratory? Do we calculate a woman's value according to the potential economic impact of a loss of life or limb? Can we assign a woman value according to the bride-price a man would pay to marry her?

We would perform calculations as cold and callous as these for a used car or any other type of machine, perhaps, but never for a woman. That's because a woman's value, just like the value of every human being, is immeasurable. But how many women realize their true worth?

> A WOMAN'S VALUE, JUST LIKE THE
> VALUE OF EVERY HUMAN BEING,
> IS IMMEASURABLE.

INNATELY AND INESTIMABLY VALUABLE

One reason for your inestimable value is your utter uniqueness. No one can debate that you are unique, an unmatched part of God's creation.

There are five elements that distinguish every human being in a unique combination that is unrepeatable. Those elements are: (1) the physical; (2) the characteristics of your personality;

(3) your social experience; (4) your intellect; and (5) your spirituality.

1. **The physical.** No one is physically identical to you. Even in monozygotic twins, who share 100 percent of their genetic load, one can differentiate between the two based on such unique characteristics as scars, hairstyles, moles and freckles, and other elements, which means that no matter how similar you may be to another person, your physique and your anatomy will not be repeated.

2. **The characteristics of your personality.** Your perspectives, points of view, the experiences you have lived, your joys, your sorrows, and your abilities are grouped uniquely in you. No one has the exact combination of these elements that make up your personality.

3. **Your social experience.** Your way of relating to others—especially as it concerns your emotions and feelings—is not repeated in another human being. We are born into a world where we encounter other people and exchange ideas, experiences, and affection. None of your family members, friends, neighbors, classmates, or coworkers has a relationship with you that perfectly matches your relationship with anyone else. Mothers of multiple children are not even the same mother for each child. I have four daughters, and my experience raising each one of them is distinctly unique.

4. **Your intellect.** The skills and abilities that we develop in our minds and inner selves are also unique. People who have the same IQ are not equally intelligent. Our willingness to learn and our intellectual interests are not repeated. In the areas of logical-mathematical, spatial, musical, kinesthetic, intrapersonal, interpersonal, and emotional intelligences, no two people

in the world possess the identical combination of these multiple intelligences.

5. **Your spirituality.** Your relationship with God is also unique. What there is of God in each one of us, since we were made in His image and likeness (see Genesis 1:26–27), is also unique.

The value of a real flesh-and-blood woman, combined with her experiences and the elements that make up her being, cannot be quantified with all the money in the world because she is unique and unrepeatable. If we can call a piece of man-made artwork "priceless," if we can assign exorbitant worth to houses, cars, and boats, then why do we find it so hard to understand that, as women created by the one true Artist, our value is incalculable? Remember, that very Artist paid the incalculable price for the salvation of our souls on Calvary. He paid the price for each person, thereby ascribing immeasurable value to every human being on the planet.

We weren't created by chance. If we internalize our value by acknowledging these principles, we can certainly rise to become the women we aspire to be, rather than settling for a devalued version of ourselves.

Even if your life has not
followed the path you would
have preferred, you are valuable
in a way that never changes.

Chapter 2

MISTAKEN PREREQUISITES FOR POSSESSING VALUE

*W*hen I first enrolled in college, I was studying at the largest university on my island. There was an expansive hall in one building where walls were lined with posters listing the various courses, schedules, professors, and materials needed. Not every class was offered every semester, and when I started, the other freshmen and I got the last pick. As I filled out my schedule, I noticed a listing for a course that seemed to fit perfectly with the others I had already chosen for the upcoming semester. But when I went to enroll for that particular course, I was denied entry. The registrar informed me that I had not fulfilled the class prerequisite. I didn't understand until then that all those "perfect-sounding" classes required the completion of other, more elementary, freshman-level courses. Thank goodness there are no prerequisites for being valuable! Unfortunately, many women carry over the concept of prerequisites to their worth, mistakenly thinking there are conditions they must meet or accomplishments they need to achieve for them to be considered valuable and worthy. And it's no wonder this idea is so prevalent because women find themselves under continual pressure to conform to the expectations of others—whether family members, friends, or society as a whole.

As daughters, we are expected to be obedient and submissive; young girls often strive harder to achieve grace and beauty than to develop their intellectual abilities. In many parts of the world, despite recent advances in equal rights for both sexes, women are still educated to believe that getting married, raising children, and managing a household are the ultimate expression of their potential. Decorum and submissiveness in behavior are highly praised, often above any other type of accomplishment. And within a family, even if a woman does not work outside the home, she bears the brunt of pressures associated with raising children and keeping a house. Unlike men, of whom the primary expectation is to have a job and be a faithful provider for their family, women have countless expectations imposed on them involving the care of the home, the children, and extended family.

While I do not offer unqualified support to the feminist movement, I am grateful to those voices that have exposed the people and institutions reinforcing a fixed ideal of how a woman's life should be. At the same time, I need to point out that while marriage and family can impose a significant number of expectations on women, there are plenty of women whose genuine desire is to fulfill those expectations, to meet those standards. And there is nothing wrong with that. As long as a woman is free to pursue that which fulfills her—the role God has called her to, and for which He has equipped her—whatever she may choose is legitimate, and *she has value regardless.*

The following are some factors that many women seem to believe are necessary for them to have value. They forget, or never realize, that their value is inherent and does not depend at all on these things but only on the One who created them to be totally and utterly unique.

> AS LONG AS A WOMAN IS FREE TO PURSUE THAT WHICH FULFILLS HER, WHATEVER SHE MAY CHOOSE IS LEGITIMATE, AND *SHE HAS VALUE REGARDLESS.*

FORMAL EDUCATION

You do not need a formal education, validated by diplomas and degrees, to be valuable. Now, I don't discount the importance of education. I encourage every woman to study, learn new things, and enrich her knowledge. Earning a diploma or a university degree makes a difference in the pay you'll receive for performing a job and even the positions you can apply for in your life. However, formal education does not determine the value of a woman.

A woman who lacks formal education is no less valuable than one who holds multiple degrees because measures of intellect or academic accomplishments don't determine a woman's value. If you dream about studying and pursuing a degree, don't delay; but understand that a diploma will not raise your value.

Women today have unprecedented opportunities in academia. Our ancestors didn't have any of the advantages that you and I enjoy today. But please understand that even if you don't pursue a degree or earn outstanding academic achievements, you are still worthy! Exercise your intelligence to the fullest, but don't fall for the lie that says you are worth only as much as the degrees you've earned.

NOTEWORTHY SOCIAL CONTRIBUTIONS

You do not need to be a renowned philanthropist or a decorated community volunteer to have value. The beneficial contributions we make to our neighborhood, community, church, workplace, and so forth are highly valuable, of course, but they have no bearing on our value as individuals.

I believe every woman should use her God-given talents to benefit her local community and promote the well-being of her people. I thank God for the hundreds of women who have worked with me on social causes. I applaud every woman who sows her time, talents, and financial resources into her church, her local community, her children's school, and so forth. I am sure that the law of sowing and reaping (see, for example, Galatians 6:7) will bear fruit and increase in each of these women's lives. Their contributions are essential and add tremendous value to society and the places that are impacted by their help. But that doesn't make those women more valuable.

BEING MARRIED

Many women see marital status as a significant indicator of their value. For some reason, the life of a single woman is often painted as being a sad, lonely, and flawed existence. Unfortunately, in many cases, that impression turns into a self-fulfilling prophecy for women who idealize marriage to the extent that they refuse to feel joyful or content until they've found a husband.

I always desired to get married. Otoniel and I have been married for almost three decades, and I thank the Lord that I found my partner at a young age. However, such is not necessarily the case for every woman who wishes to get married. Nor is it true that every heterosexual woman desires to have a husband, though there are probably many women who fail to recognize their lack of desire.

BEWARE THE PRESSURE TO MARRY

Although the world by and large no longer perceives marriage and motherhood as the sole purposes of a woman's existence, many women still believe that they are "nothing" without a husband or children. Questions such as "Do you have a boyfriend?" and "Any special guy in your life?" are asked of almost every woman starting at a young age. Little girls spend hours fantasizing about their dream wedding—often launching a lifelong obsession that they can't abandon until they hear wedding bells. Our culture instills in the minds of young girls—through fairy tales, romantic movies, and other influences—the belief that getting married is the end-all, be-all for any young woman. Many women idolize sparkly engagement rings, elegant wedding dresses, elaborate marriage ceremonies, and exotic honeymoons so much that they rush into marriage with the wrong person. Settling for someone rather than waiting patiently for the man God intends for them can be a mistake—*if* He intends for them to marry.

JOY IS POSSIBLE FOR SINGLE WOMEN

The truth is, a woman can live a joyful life as a single lady. Never let anyone measure your value based on whether or not you have a marriage partner. You are worthy on your own. If you are single, celebrate your singleness and determine to live life to the fullest. Realize that you can be a dignified, joy-filled woman without a man by your side. Think of the women who were once married but are now divorced or widowed and do not wish to remarry. Their choice is legitimate. Sure, God said, "It is not good that man should be alone" (Genesis 2:18), but He made no similar comments about the woman. The life of a single woman can be imbued with purpose, no matter her age. (See, for example, Titus 2:4.)

When my grandmother died, my grandfather remarried three months later, much to the chagrin of my aunts. I could see, however, that for my grandfather, it was tough to live alone after spending so many years with my grandmother as a constant companion and help. The companionship of a woman was something he needed. Had it been my grandfather who passed first, I don't believe my grandmother would have hoped to remarry. I don't say this because I think women are stronger or more self-reliant than men; I only think that my grandmother would have seen singleness as an opportunity to invest more time and energy into the lives of her children and grandchildren.

My point is that there are women who have found genuine contentment without a husband, whether they never married or were widowed. We aren't living in Bible times, when getting married and giving birth were the highest callings of a woman— essentially all she could aspire to unless she was a priestess or a prophetess. Our society is not that of the Old Testament, when having an abundance of offspring was an indication of divine favor and blessing, and when a woman was a piece of property, belonging first to her father and then passing hands to her husband upon marriage.

ESCAPE THE STIGMA OF SINGLENESS

Unfortunately, in some contexts, unmarried women are looked down upon and treated as inferior; if they are not made to feel discarded, they are treated as a threat to others' marriages. After two-plus decades in pastoral ministry, I have met with many women who were frustrated, desperate, and depressed because of their lack of a partner. Even worse, I have witnessed women leaving one toxic relationship, only to enter immediately into another relationship that is equally toxic, if not more so, just to avoid being alone. The idea that a woman without a husband and children has diminished value remains embedded in the minds of many. Even though this myth has been debunked and has even disappeared in many contexts, it persists enough to plague a significant number of women, leading them to believe that without a man or children, their lives have no meaning. How many women put their lives on hold, delaying their dreams for the sake of their search for a spouse?

HAVING A HUSBAND AND CHILDREN IS NOT A PREREQUISITE TO YOUR HAVING VALUE.

Now, I am a staunch defender of marriage. I believe that the union between husband and wife is sacred. And I aspired to get married, but my life didn't stop while I was waiting for a husband to drop into my lap. Likewise, no woman should stop her life in order to search for a husband.

Again, having a husband and children is not a prerequisite to your having value. Your life has a purpose from the very beginning, not beginning with your wedding day. Single women and married women without children have just as much value as married women and mothers, and their dreams are just as worthy.

FINANCIAL WEALTH OR MATERIAL POSSESSIONS

Some equate value with material possessions and wealth. Impressive investment portfolios, brand-name items, large houses, multiple properties, expensive cars—none of these is a sign of any individual's worth. Don't get me wrong; I am not saying that any of those things is inherently wrong. Prosperity is a blessing that need not taint our character. I make this clarification because I have been targeted by many who claim that their humble resources prove their humility of character. Those who view any aspirations of wealth or prestige as sinful do not have a sound understanding of biblical humility. I don't know about you, but I want to be the best that I can be in every area of life as a way to bring glory to my Maker, and that includes in the area of my finances.

It is human nature to desire the best things, and that is because we were made in the image of God, who likewise desires good things for His children. *"Let the LORD be magnified, who has pleasure in the prosperity of His servant"* (Psalm 35:27). This desire for good things, for our benefit, is a natural, God-given desire. If you were to ask a young child which toy he would prefer—a cutting-edge remote-control car with bright lights, realistic sound effects, and other fancy features, or a wooden vehicle that's worn to the point of breaking—would you call him selfish and lacking in humility if he picked the newer, functioning toy? Of course not! Children can distinguish between good and evil in their human nature, and we don't fault them for choosing the good. Why should we condemn ourselves for doing the same thing?

Again, there is no inherent sin in wanting or working for good things. It's a gift from God to be able to acquire wealth and material possessions. At the same time, we have to understand that material possessions are not a sign of our value. Your car, your house, your luxury items can make your life easier. They can elevate your social status, and they can signal just how hard you've strived and worked, but they will never be a reflection of your value. Your value does not correlate with your wealth.

PERSONAL ACHIEVEMENTS

Many women may congratulate themselves for being free of the pressure to marry or the insatiable hunger for material possessions, never realizing that they have fallen prey to a different determination of their worth: personal achievements. These are the women who shrug off the fact that they're single, but only because they can "fall back on their laurels" and comfort themselves with reminders of their career success and professional accomplishments. The truth is, personal achievements do not garner us any additional worth. Some women dedicate themselves, body and soul, to their careers; they claim that marriage and children would hinder their growth, so they reject these things completely. While there is nothing inherently wrong with striving for professional achievements, I caution you not to equate career success with value.

Many people ascribe more significant value to careers that bring in more money or require more years of schooling and training than others. But is a female CEO any better than the woman who cleans the office? I recognize the effort, dedication, and sacrifices that many women have made to occupy an executive position or start their own business. Still, our worth is not a measure of those sacrifices and efforts.

I know personally the great sacrifices that must be made by a woman who prioritizes her family and her career. I have held management positions in distinguished private companies throughout my professional life, and I have always strived to glorify God through my work. Each of my professional roles has blessed me, taught me, and shaped me in significant ways. But I am under no false impression; I realize that the absence of these experiences would not make me any less valuable. I once gave up a position that had taken me a lot of effort to secure. I did this because I was getting married. But since I already understood my value and its true source, I felt no loss of worth as I transitioned for a season from the corporate world to the domestic sphere. I knew what would be best for that chapter of my life, and I acted accordingly, never doubting my worth or feeling that, by getting married, I was compromising my value.

ABSOLUTE VALUE

I cannot accept, promote, or participate in the erroneous thinking that certain attributes or achievements can make one person more valuable than another or can even increase a person's value relative to what it once was. Each of us is entitled to celebrate our accomplishments, but let's not allow ourselves to feel a sense of inflated value because of them. Along the same lines, if we fall short of reaching a goal we have set, or if we lack the advantages and resources that might have secured us a certain position of prestige, let's not wallow in feelings of inferiority, forgetting that our value is set and unchangeable. So, celebrate your decisions, your achievements, and your position along your life's journey, valuing yourself for who you are and where you are, no matter if there is a place you would rather be or something else you would rather do.

As you learn to value yourself regardless of your circumstances, be sure to work on extending the same attitude toward other women rather than either envying them or looking down on them. Respect your fellow sisters and celebrate their journey, regardless of their successes and failures. When it comes to life choices, avoid judging other women for making decisions differently than you do. Each of us has a unique purpose and a personalized set of goals that support that purpose. If you are married with children, don't let yourself feel any more or less valuable than, say, your neighbor who is married but, rather than start a family, pursued her career and has amassed a long list of professional degrees and titles. If you are a career-minded woman who has chosen not to marry or have children, don't look with contempt upon women who have left the career track to stay home with their kids.

EACH OF US HAS A UNIQUE PURPOSE AND A PERSONALIZED SET OF GOALS THAT SUPPORT THAT PURPOSE.

Just as we are all unique and unrepeatable, our decisions and paths are unique and unrepeatable. Understand that your value is unconditional and independent of your academic accomplishments, marital status, possessions, personal achievements, and other factors. It is only when you value yourself where you are, for who you are and what you have, that you gain the freedom to pursue your deepest desires and wildest dreams. But even the fulfillment of those desires and dreams will not alter your value one bit. Take heart! Even if your life has not followed the path you would have preferred, you are valuable in a way that never changes. Because your Creator has endued you with purpose and value, you can be content with yourself where you are, even as you continue to chase after the call He has placed within you.

As we will see in the next chapter, the pursuit of one's call is never without challenges, especially in a world where the expectations placed on women are demanding and diverse. The good news is, you have what it takes to break the mold, drown out the voices that would detain you, and discover just what it is you most deeply desire to do.

As women, we have to
decide that our gender will
not define what we can do
or who we should be.

DREAMING IN A WORLD OF DOUBLE STANDARDS

J once counseled a divorced mother who explained how she had decided to let her ex-husband have custody of their son during the week, while she would have custody on weekends alone. She said she didn't want her relationship with her son to be dominated by the daily grind of waking early, going to school, doing homework, and other weekday commitments. Her decision was to let her ex-husband handle all those responsibilities so that she could handle the "pleasant" parts of parenting on the weekends: fun outings, sports activities, and so forth.

When our conversation ended, I confess that I judged this woman's parenting skills. But after further reflection, I realized that I knew plenty of divorced mothers whose hearts were broken because they acted as primary caregivers for their children—shuttling the kids to their activities, sacrificing for them, and helping them through the mundane and sometimes unpleasant realities of daily life—only to hear those children express a preference to "spend time with Daddy." It's true that in many families affected by separations and divorce, the father becomes a "Disney dad," having custody of the kids on weekends and cramming their schedule with only fun activities and no responsibilities. In most cases, it's Mom, not Dad, directing the kids on a daily basis to pick up their shoes, take a bath, do their homework, and so on. Upon recognizing this trend, I applauded this divorced mother for choosing what she understood to be the best arrangement for her and, therefore, for her son.

Trends such as this have a tremendous influence on the decisions women make today. Sadly, many women orient themselves and their desires primarily around what is expected of them—by their families, by their employers, and by society in general. Whether by outright manipulation or subtle influence, these outside voices speak into these women's lives, often dictating their dreams and even limiting their potential. Let's explore some of the ways in which women are subject to outside influences that can threaten to derail their desires.

EMOTIONAL MANIPULATION

Women are known for being compassionate people, having a heart for those in need. Yet this empathetic nature can be an Achilles' heel when other people play upon it, asking for help or simply acting incapable of doing something on their own. It is often assumed that a woman will let go of her desires to benefit the best interests of her husband and children and make endless sacrifices to meet her family's every need. Whether overt or unconscious, this type of manipulation constitutes emotional blackmail and can put a permanent damper on a woman's dreams.

TRAPPED BY GUILT

Emotional manipulation preys in particular upon women's tendency to guilt-trip themselves. An immense sense of guilt burdens many women, sometimes over a mistake they made and even sometimes over a decision they made that benefited them, as if they didn't deserve to be blessed. The guilt that stems from an awareness of a mistake that we made is something we first experienced in childhood when our parents pointed out our errors to help us grow into responsible people of impeccable character. In this sense, as an operation of our moral conscience, guilt can be a healthy, even helpful, experience.

Why is guilt so frequently a "female problem"? The answer lies in the foundations of humanity in the garden of Eden. According to the biblical record, the woman first ate the forbidden fruit, which she then shared with her husband. (See Genesis 3.) Even though it was the man, not the woman, who received the warning about the fruit in the first place, the woman has forever borne the blame for introducing sin into the world for all eternity. Eve was hardly alone in her iniquity—Adam and the serpent were equally at fault and were penalized along with Eve—yet the responsibility for the first sin is always placed on Eve, in particular, and all women in general.

Though guilt can sometimes be productive in guiding us to good behavior, guilt ceases to be beneficial when it brings on the self-destructive attitude of shame and the emotional and even physical hurt that can result. As a faculty of imperfection, shame can cause women to feel that they are without value and to lose hope of ever remedying the problem; in many cases, they will continue making the same mistake that led to the guilt and shame in the first place.

ENSLAVED BY SHAME

This vicious cycle of guilt and shame traps many women in an endless sequence of unhealthy relationships. A woman who finds herself in an abusive relationship, for example, may experience guilt over choosing the wrong partner. A woman who has a child outside of wedlock may experience guilt for her choice and also on behalf of her children if those kids grow up without a father. The intensity of guilt and shame can be the difference between a woman saying "I am facing a disaster" and "I *am* a disaster."

Shame tells you that you're bad because you've done something wrong. It often correlates with substance abuse and addiction, depression, bullying, eating disorders, violence, aggression, and thoughts of suicide. These types of troubles afflict millions of women worldwide. It may well be that you have experienced one or more of them or that they are plaguing someone close to you.

When a shame mentality takes hold, a woman may accept critical comments, physical and emotional abuse, inappropriate behaviors, and other adverse treatment from a partner because she thinks she deserves such treatment. She says to herself, "I can't have a good life. I don't deserve to be happy. I'm useless."

For men, the experience of shame is usually far more straightforward: it comes down to being told they are weak because weakness is the root of shame for most men. A man may experience embarrassment and shame over an obvious shortcoming, such as infertility, hair loss, or a lack of finesse for a sport or athletic endeavor. On the other hand, women may experience guilt and shame over any number of issues—often because they can't be and do it all! The so-called "weaker sex" is expected to be capable, well-rounded, and far stronger in their endeavors. Many women feel an intense burden to exhibit nothing short of perfection in every aspect of life—physique, household, marriage, children, career—and when the inevitable occurs and she falls short, the resulting shame can be crippling.

SEXUALITY AND SEDUCTION

One of the most glaring double standards exists in the world of sexuality. By and large, men are encouraged, even expected, to have sexual experiences from an early age and out of wedlock; a lack of sexual experience often equates to weakness. Meanwhile, the opposite is true for women: they are expected to keep themselves virtuous and pure. Any early forays into the sexual experience are seen to taint their sexual allure permanently.

In the absence of her virginity, a woman is often treated as a second-class citizen. She is dismissed as worthless, "loose," and "trashy." In my years of ministry, I have met many women who were victims of contempt and humiliation because of hasty, unchaste decisions they made early on. Some of these women were not careful because they lacked an adequate education on sexuality and did not know any better. Others were deceived and manipulated by a man who demanded sex as proof of affection or falsely promised to be faithful forever. In the end, these women were left feeling used and discarded—and emotionally scarred.

When a marriage falls apart, in most cases, the woman is blamed—either for infidelity or, if it was the husband who was unfaithful, for failing to give him adequate love, attention, and respect, resulting in his looking to someone else to meet those needs of his. When people hear about a couple separating or divorcing, the question is raised, "Why couldn't so and so hold on to her man?" In biblical times, a man could divorce a woman for any reason whatsoever, and he wasn't expected to be faithful. The only way a woman could get out of a marriage was by becoming a widow, and if she was found being unfaithful, she was killed.

In John 8, we find a telling story of a woman caught in adultery. Jesus was teaching in the temple at Jerusalem when the local scribes and Pharisees came and threw before Him a woman they reported to have been caught in adultery, saying, "*Teacher, this woman was caught in adultery, in the very act*" (John 8:4). "Caught in the act"? That means they would have known the identity of the man with whom she had been unfaithful, and yet that particular man received no mention, no accusation, and no sentence. Faultfinding fingers were pointed at the woman alone.

Fortunately, the woman was spared being stoned because Jesus was there to prick the consciences of these self-righteous scribes and Pharisees. (See verses 6–9.) Yet, we are reminded that when it comes to marriages plagued by sexual dalliance and ending in divorce, blame often falls to the woman, even though marriage is meant to be a partnership with both spouses bearing equal responsibility for marital fidelity.

TRADITIONAL GENDER ROLES IN THE HOUSEHOLD

I get angry when I hear a married woman using the phrase "babysitting" to describe what her husband does when she leaves their children at home with him. A father is just as responsible as a mother for the needs and welfare of his children. So, don't offer any extra praise for a dad who changes a diaper! The baby is his just as much as his wife's. In my household, there are two adults—my husband and I—responsible for the lives of our four children. We both raise them. We both educate them. We are both responsible for them. In the absence of one parent, the other parent is entirely in charge (and isn't "babysitting").

Just as we cannot continue to foster the idea that fathers are caregivers of their children only in the mother's absence, we shouldn't entertain the belief that specific roles belong in either the male or female sphere. For example, cooking meals is often associated with girls and women; but shouldn't we all have the ability to feed ourselves? All children, regardless of gender, should receive instruction in personal hygiene, home upkeep, fiscal responsibility, and other disciplines.

WE SHOULDN'T ENTERTAIN THE BELIEF THAT SPECIFIC ROLES BELONG IN EITHER THE MALE OR FEMALE SPHERE.

When it comes to assigning household chores, the idea that girls should cook, clean, and do laundry indoors while boys should take out the trash and handle the yard work is entirely wrong. Everyone should know how to scrub and how to take out the garbage. Everyone should be able to cook a meal and clean a load of laundry. Is a woman any less female for painting a fence or cutting the grass? Is a man any less male for ironing clothes or baking a cake? Women and men may be fundamentally different, biologically speaking, but there's no genetic rule governing the household tasks they're capable of performing.

A woman may be made to feel inferior or unworthy if she decides that motherhood is not for her or if she dislikes cooking. These long-held views of activities that belong to the "woman's sphere" have kept many women in bondage and prevented them from pursuing their heart's deepest desires.

POVERTY AND GENDER DISCREPANCIES IN WAGES

In the United States, poverty affects women more than men.[2] Globally, in almost all regions, it's recorded that women live at higher poverty rates.[3] Of course, this figure relates that many women, if they leave the workforce when they have children, and even before then, do not generate a fixed income. Countless women have had to decide between their career and their family—a dilemma that rarely affects men. And the stigma of their decision can weigh heavily on women or even make them feel guilty for not "choosing" the other option.

In addition to having lesser representation in the global workforce, women carry out the majority of unpaid jobs, such as volunteer work and home care. In the United States alone, "women perform an average of four hours of unpaid work per day compared to men's two and a half hours," mainly in the home.[4] From gender discrepancies in earnings to the difficult decision of career or family, many women face a great deal of frustration when it comes to their work. A woman in a state of

2. Robin Bleiweis, Diana Boesch, and Alexandra Cawthorne Gaines, "The Basic Facts About Women in Poverty," August 3, 2020, Center for American Progress, https://www.americanprogress.org/issues/women/reports/2020/08/03/488536/ basic-facts-women-poverty/.
3. See, for example, "Why the majority of the world's poor are women," OXFAM International, https://www.oxfam.org/en/why-majority-worlds-poor-are-women.
4. Gus Wezerek and Kristen R. Ghodsee, "Women's Unpaid Labor is Worth $10,900,000,000,000," *The New York Times* online, March 5, 2020, https://www.nytimes.com/interactive/2020/03/04/opinion/women-unpaid-labor.html.

true poverty may feel utterly unworthy. Many women devalue themselves for not being able to sustain themselves financially and failing to meet the needs of their families. Their economic situation may adversely affect the way they value themselves.

SOCIAL PRESSURES

Many forces in our society reduce women to sexual objects. I think mainly about the popularity of songs denigrating the female sex. On the other hand, the cry of feminism, which seeks to elevate women, often provokes an effect opposite of its intentions, resulting in the devaluation of women. In championing the idea that women can do anything, this viewpoint casts a negative light on traditional women's roles and any woman who legitimately desires to fulfill those roles.

Speaking of women's roles, a woman who elects to stay home, with or without children to raise, may feel a sense of shame and guilt over not holding a job or making financial contributions to her household. But the career woman is not exempt from shame, either, if she feels convicted for taking time away from her husband, her children, and her home as she devotes herself to her work. Finding a balance between work and family is a massive challenge for many women.

A good friend of mine started her own business in a different country from where she was born. She was single when she started, and once she got married and gave birth to her first child, everything changed. One day when we got together, she confessed that she was feeling conflicted, caught between the warring desires to continue working as an entrepreneur and dedicating herself 100 percent to her family. I advised her to do what she believed would bring her more satisfaction and a more significant benefit for the future of everyone involved.

Unfortunately, many women don't have the luxury of making this decision; it may well be that their family's financial situation requires them to continue working and to place their children in daycare—often causing even more guilt, as we've discussed.

THE PRESSURE TO PURSUE BEAUTY AND AN ATTRACTIVE PHYSIQUE

Most women also experience intense pressure regarding their physical appearance. Compared to the idealized, photoshopped images of models and movie stars, many women feel their physical imperfections magnified to the extent that it causes them shame. Some women struggle their entire lives to reach a place of contentment with their weight, their jean size, their complexion, their hairstyle, and so forth. Some women think they're too chubby; others are told they're too skinny. Those with straight hair wish they had curls; those with curly hair would do anything to straighten it permanently.

Tell me, what are the critical concerns of men when it comes to their physical appearance? Muscles and hair growth, perhaps. But women feel scrutinized in every category, from fitness level to fashion sense. No wonder so many of them battle insecurities and low self-esteem.

POLITICAL UNFAIRNESS

Women rarely get equal representation with men in the political sphere, meaning that, in many cases, the interests and needs of the female sex are not taken into account. But when women participate in politics at any level, more attention is given to such realms as health, education, and civil rights. The World Economic Forum has reported a positive relationship between women in elected political positions and their participation in the workforce. In an article published by the organization, the authors assert, "We believe that electing more women in government not only promotes gender equality and strengthens democratic institutions but also makes real and substantive contributions to government spending and population health."[5] When women are politically involved, the economic situation of all women in that nation improves as a result of their participation.

SILENCING THE VOICES THAT DEVALUE US

When we consider the above, we realize that women are constantly receiving conflicting messages about their worth. And nobody would dispute the fact that women have long been considered inferior to men. Which of these deep-seated beliefs or traditional perspectives has shaped the way you value yourself?

As women, we have to decide that our gender will not prescribe what we can do or who we should be. Outside of motherhood, which is reserved exclusively for women by nature, it's up to us to decide which roles we will occupy within our family, neighborhood, society, workforce, political sphere, and so forth. Regardless of any parameters that seem to have been established in your sphere of life regarding what you can or cannot do, the truth is that *you're the one who must decide.*

I am the proud mother of four daughters, and one of the most important things I have instilled in them is the importance of pursuing their abilities, dreams, and desires without any ear to what society may have to say about things they "should" or "shouldn't" do.

As women, we cannot continue to promote these traditionalist views when we know how they are reducing our value,

---

5. Carles Muntaner and Edwin Ng, "Here's why having more women in government is good for your health," World Economic Forum online, January 16, 2019, https://www.weforum.org/agenda/2019/01/the-more-women-in-government-the-healthier-a-population.

whether in others' eyes or our own. We have to change the way we see what we've been taught, and we have to renew our minds accordingly. Above all, we must learn to position ourselves correctly.

AS WOMEN, WE HAVE TO CHANGE
THE WAY WE SEE WHAT WE'VE BEEN
TAUGHT, AND WE HAVE TO RENEW OUR
MINDS ACCORDINGLY.

"YOU CAN'T CHOOSE YOUR FAMILY"— OR CAN YOU?

People often repeat the truism "You can't choose your family." It sounds very philosophical, but I would contend that it is only halfway valid. True, you can't choose your parents or your siblings. But you can—and you will—choose the family you will have, from your spouse to your children to your grandchildren. With some exceptions in certain cultures, of course, most of us indeed have the freedom to choose our marriage partner. While many people will encounter resistance from their parents over the person they want to marry, it is no longer common for parents to arrange marriages for their children. Likewise, whether or not you have children, and the number of children you have, is primarily up to you and your spouse. The same is true of the neighborhood you choose to raise them in, the educational path you select for them, the values you instill in them, and so forth. You didn't choose the family you were born into, but you get to choose the family you will build.

When internalized at a young age, this truth can produce a powerfully positive impact on a young woman's future.

Whenever I meet someone single, I caution him or her, "Choose well who you marry. Think carefully about who you are going to start a family with." In the school that our church hosts, there are many family situations represented. I have comforted children who were crying tears of disappointment because their father or mother broke their promise to attend a specific activity or program. I've made exceptions for frustrated mothers who have shown up at the office pleading for an extension on a payment deadline because they didn't receive their alimony check on time. I've sent acceptance letters to students with transcripts and performance evaluations that weren't up to par with our usual expectations because I knew that their parents were separating or getting a divorce. I know the emotional toll those kinds of ruptures can take on a child. Each of these situations is a learning opportunity for a young person who has not yet formed a family. I don't want to plant seeds of fear regarding the commitment of marriage. Still, I want to encourage young people to seek suitable characteristics in the partner with whom they decide to start a family.

Some of you may be saying, "What do I do when the decisions have already been made? I've gotten married! I have children! Is it too late for me?" Don't despair. There is still hope for you to obtain the results you expect. I believe that change is always possible when we have faith, when we take our troubles to the Lord in prayer, and when we seek divine wisdom for our decisions. We will discuss all these areas in upcoming chapters.

CHOOSE YOUR OWN RULES AND ROLES

As for your family, find your place—the one you want to occupy with the roles you want to fulfill. If you like cooking, do it, enjoy it. If you don't like cooking, let someone else do it. If you enjoy cooking and cook regularly, never devalue a woman who does not share your passion. Likewise, if you don't enjoy cooking, never devalue a woman who does.

If you want to get married, get married, be happy. Suppose you don't want to get married, good for you. Enjoy your singleness.

If you want to have children, do it, whether through natural means or the process of adoption. If you don't want to have children, live life to the fullest, and don't listen to anyone who may nag you about the ever-decreasing productive time that your uterus has left.

As for society, don't applaud the wrong agendas. Not only do we need more women in politics, but we also need women who represent us all, not just those who denigrate men and prioritize such liberal policies as abortion. Let's likewise stand firm and not promote any misogynistic messages.

In the workforce, strive to go as high as you can. Even with the gender inequality that remains in the workforce, the truth is that it is more feasible today than ever for women to attain high positions in corporations, nonprofits, and other types of businesses. Aspire to the highest position, if you wish. If you have a family, don't feel that you have to stop working and stay home. If you can make suitable childcare arrangements, then do so.

I thank God that my husband and our daughters have given me space and support to grow and develop spiritually and professionally. By His grace, I have not had to struggle against family resistance, as many other women do. It has certainly helped that I have always promoted, with my husband and children, a fair mentality toward women's roles and an openness to personal dreams. I decided long ago that I would not allow my daughters to become victims of the dictates of society concerning gender roles. It has been an unspeakable blessing to model for them the freedom they have to follow their dreams, and I pray that you, too, will cast off any restrictions keeping you from valuing yourself and going after your vision.

How often is it

that our own negative

thoughts and unhealthy

self-image, rather than actual

rejection by a person or an

organization, hold us back?

Chapter 4

DON'T DEVALUE YOURSELF

A woman came to see me at my office at the church one day. Crying disconsolately, she told me her husband of over twenty years had just left her for another woman. She felt aimless and abandoned and didn't know what would become of her future. She had dedicated herself, body and soul, to him, to his children, to his house. "Pastor, I would iron everything for that man, even his underpants," she wailed.

When I asked her about their twenty-year relationship, she painted me a verbal picture of abuse, humiliation, and unhappiness. I was shocked because her anguish and despair seemed appropriate only if she had just lost a good man she loved very much.

Let me pause here to clarify that I am in no way saying that men are always the ones who mistreat women and take advantage of them. This scenario easily could have been reversed. Nor do I in any way advocate giving up on marriage over a disagreement or an affair. If the husband and wife can work things out, they should.

In this case, I honestly did not understand the sense of despair this woman was feeling over the departure of a man who did not appreciate her. To me, it would have made more sense for her to have felt relief when her abusive husband walked out. But it was only the moment he left, clearly intending never to return, that she sought help—it wasn't when he hit her, when he cheated on her with other women, or when he denigrated her with his words. She had tolerated that kind of behavior for two decades because of being married to him, ungrateful and unkind as he was. However, he provided this woman with a sense of purpose, of value. In her eyes, her value vanished the day her marriage ended.

The reality is that her value never left, but, for years, she had suppressed it and subjected it to the fear, guilt, shame, melancholy, depression, and rejection that characterized her marriage. The saddest thing is when a woman tolerates this kind of treatment and starts to believe she has no value without a man or without whatever it is that she's been basing her self-worth on.

Nobody can reduce or remove your value, but you can forfeit your value. You forfeit your value when you put up with harsh words, physical blows, chronic falsehoods, successive infidelities—whatever it is that you tolerate and even expect because it's become part of the foundation of your identity.

What negative, abusive, degrading experiences have marked your life? Who or what has made you feel worthless, helpless, or a waste of time? Whose words have scarred your self-esteem, diminishing your value in your mind? Who has lifted a hand to mistreat you or raised a voice in verbal abuse? What have been the circumstances that have left you exposed, feeling naked, ashamed, and hopeless? In what areas do you berate yourself the most severely for your imperfections and flaws? *When did you start believing that you're not worth it?* The answers to these questions matter a lot if you're going to destroy the illusion that your value is gone and that your dreams are unreachable and unwarranted.

> NOBODY CAN REDUCE OR REMOVE YOUR VALUE, BUT YOU CAN FORFEIT YOUR VALUE WHEN YOU PUT UP WITH WHATEVER IT IS THAT YOU TOLERATE AND EVEN EXPECT BECAUSE IT'S BECOME PART OF THE FOUNDATION OF YOUR IDENTITY.

WEATHERING REJECTION

I once heard one of my daughters—then eight years old—crying inconsolably, and I quickly went to investigate the reason for her tears. I assumed she had fallen and injured herself. I found her unscathed and soon learned that she was crying because a friend of hers was having a birthday party and had invited everyone else in the class—except for my daughter. The sting of exclusion was more than her eight-year-old heart could bear.

As a parent, I was tempted to shrug off the slight, knowing that my daughter was not likely to remember this particular instance of rejection when she grew older. Being excluded from a birthday party is hardly the end of the world. But, for my daughter, at that moment, the sting of rejection was almost as potent as physical pain. The feeling was intense, and the wound went deep.

Her experience is affirmed by a study done in 2011 on the effects of social rejection. According to the team that conducted the study, "the same regions of the brain that become active in response to painful sensory experiences are activated during intense experiences of social rejection."[6] The pain of rejection is real, and the anguish it causes can be even harder to bear than actual physical injury.

PARENTAL REJECTION

The pain of rejection is often magnified when the person doing the rejecting is one's family member or close friend. I have seen raw pain in the eyes of many women I have counseled over the years I've spent in ministry, a countless number of whom confessed to me that their parents devalued them and made them feel unworthy for the simple fact that they were born female. One particular young woman in ministry shared the pain she felt after having given everything to the church, only to be cast out the day her younger brother decided to pastor the church. It was clear that he was promoted to a position of greater leadership than she, despite her years of service, only because he was a man and not because of his contributions, talent, attributes, or calling. Unfairness of this kind happens in the workplace, especially in family businesses. There are many cases where male children occupy more prestigious positions than their sisters just because of their gender.

---

6. University of Michigan, "Study illuminates the 'pain' of social rejection," *Science Daily*, March 30, 2011, https://www.sciencedaily.com/releases/2011/03/110328151726.htm.

There are also many cases of mothers devaluing their daughters. Unfortunately, not all mothers want what's best for their children, and this includes their daughters. Dr. Karyl McBride, a family therapist, has written an excellent book exposing the effects of selfish, narcissistic mothers who view their children as a threat.[7] I have met mothers who felt jealous of their daughters because of their beauty, youth, and/or intelligence. These mothers confessed to devaluing their daughters by emphasizing their shortcomings and deficiencies, thereby damaging their daughters' self-esteem and sense of self-worth. Other mothers have rejected their daughters because they felt that their husbands paid more attention to the daughters than to their wives. Whatever the reason, there are widespread instances of mothers marginalizing their daughters and making them feel unworthy and unwanted, whether consciously or unconsciously.

MISTREATMENT BY SIBLINGS

Thank God for my parents, who treated me, my two sisters, and my brother as equals. In my house, each of us had a fair share of responsibilities; all of us were expected to study, work hard, and fight to achieve our dreams and desires, regardless of our gender. Even so, we girls were raised in the ways of femininity, while my brother was brought up in a way that cultivated his masculinity. My parents knew how to find a proper balance between not marginalizing us according to our gender while also infusing us with the specific traits and values of each sex.

Our siblings can have a significant impact on the way we value ourselves. In many cases, this occurs in a negative sense, and I am not exempt from having inflicted emotional scars on my siblings. When we were little, my sister, my brother, and I

7. Karyl McBride, *Will I Ever Be Good Enough?: Healing the Daughters of Narcissistic Mothers* (New York: Atria Paperback, 2008).

would taunt our youngest sister, telling her that she had been adopted after our parents had discovered her in a trash can. As kids, we thought this was the funniest joke, but my youngest sister told me when we had grown to adulthood that she suffered and cried a great deal as a child over our teasing.

Inside jokes can strengthen the bond between siblings, but they can also create deep relational rifts and cause intense pain to those who are either left outside the joke or made the butt of it.

There are many women whose family circles treat them in a way that causes them to feel like second-class citizens. Maybe their spouse is unfaithful, or their siblings leave them out of important decisions, or their children treat them like a maid, taking advantage of them and showing no respect. How do you suppose this kind of treatment affects the way a woman values herself? The more intimate a relationship, the stronger the potential impact it has on our self-worth.

REJECTION ON THE JOB

Another place where women are vulnerable to rejection is in the workplace. Many women devote their best efforts and contribute their precious time and talents to their day-to-day jobs, only to receive little to no recognition or appreciation from their boss. Promotions and pay raises can prove elusive, especially when many women are afraid to ask for them for fear of falling into the stereotype that society has painted of the "ruthless," go-getting woman. For these reasons, feelings of worthlessness and superfluity can plague women in the workplace.

Women with families are sometimes overlooked for promotions and special projects because of an apparent conflict of interests. An employer may hesitate to assign an important project to a woman with young children at home, lest she find herself in a position of being forced to put the project on hold so she can tend to a child's illness or a disciplinary problem. Women with families are less likely to be available for overtime work when needed. Their bosses may expect a lack of adequate focus because of the frequently distracting nature of children. Maternity-leave requirements may also make women with families less sought after than single women or men. But I would submit that a woman who is balancing a career and her family commitments is uniquely qualified to multitask and solve problems using creative solutions in the marketplace.

If you have felt devalued and underappreciated on the job, just remember that you should be working *"as to the Lord and not to men, knowing that from the Lord you will receive the reward of the inheritance; for you serve the Lord Christ"* (Colossians 3:23–24). Don't be like those individuals who "[love] *the praise of men more than the praise of God"* (John 12:43). Even though we naturally thrive from the positive input of others, no amount of verbal praise or recognition can compare with the value our heavenly Father places on us and our efforts to benefit His kingdom.

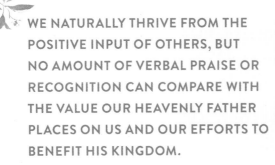

WE NATURALLY THRIVE FROM THE POSITIVE INPUT OF OTHERS, BUT NO AMOUNT OF VERBAL PRAISE OR RECOGNITION CAN COMPARE WITH THE VALUE OUR HEAVENLY FATHER PLACES ON US AND OUR EFFORTS TO BENEFIT HIS KINGDOM.

THE LANGUAGE OF REJECTION

Rejection is communicated in a variety of manners, whether overtly or via condescending words and debasing behavior. The rhyme that goes "Sticks and stones may break my bones, but words can never hurt me" could not be more wrong. In the book *Words Can Change Your Brain*, Dr. Andrew Newberg and Mark Robert Waldman explain how hostile language disrupts the production of the neurochemicals that protect us from stress. A single negative word spoken to us can activate the center of our brain in a way that unleashes the production of stress hormones and neurotransmitters, consequently disrupting the normal functioning of our brain. In this way, negative words have the power to mark us emotionally and harm us physically.[8]

I have counseled hundreds of women who described the feeling of their souls being torn when their husbands told them they no longer loved them or that they were going to leave them for another woman. Many women put up with patterns of verbal abuse from their partners—men who probably promised them love and protection at some point—never realizing just how much emotional and physical damage they are subjecting themselves to in the long run.

Positive words, on the other hand—terms such as *love* and *peace*—help the emotional centers of the brain calm down and even strengthen the frontal area of the brain, improving cognitive functioning.[9]

We should never underestimate the power of others' words to us—or of the words we speak, whether to others or ourselves. What we listen to, whether it's coming from someone

---

8. Andrew Newberg, M.D., and Mark Robert Waldman, *Words Can Change Your Brain: 12 Conversation Strategies to Build Trust, Resolve Conflict, and Increase Intimacy* (New York: Penguin Group, 2012).
9. Ibid., 27–28.

else or from deep inside of us, will largely determine the scope of our dreams and the success of our endeavors. As the writer of Proverbs put it, *"Death and life are in the power of the tongue"* (Proverbs 18:21). For every demeaning comment we hear, we need to build ourselves up again by dwelling on the truth— what God's Word says about us—and renew our commitment to speaking only in an edifying way to others so that we won't be guilty of crushing their spirits and quenching their dreams with our words.

WE SHOULD NEVER UNDERESTIMATE THE POWER OF OTHERS' WORDS TO US—OR OF THE WORDS WE SPEAK, WHETHER TO OTHERS OR OURSELVES.

REFUSE TO REPEAT

We tend to repeat what we've heard regularly, so if you were raised in a home where verbal abuse and demeaning language were the norm, it will be hard work to break this cycle. But it is possible to retrain your mind and to censor your words, especially when you rely on the power of God's Holy Spirit to help you.

Please pay close attention to your conversations with other people, keeping watch for how they react to your comments. Are you in any way repeating the verbal hurts that you have suffered? Perhaps you find that your speech denigrates your partner, parents, children, or even yourself. "But they did it to me first," you might say. No excuses! Put a stop to insulting words in any context. Break the cycle of negativity by deciding to silence any speech that isn't edifying, even if nobody has had the courtesy to do that for you. Seek to use your words only to affirm and show appreciation for your loved ones, your coworkers, your neighbors, and anyone you meet.

EXTEND FORGIVENESS

A pastor friend of mine had an ailing uncle whom she supported through his most challenging days and even sustained him financially until his death. When I learned that this man had sexually abused her as a child, I had to ask her how she managed to extend such care to someone who had inflicted so much pain on her and severely devalued her. She replied, "I forgave him. I understood that his behavior toward me was wrong, but that I didn't have to live with his mistakes, and if I didn't forgive, I would live with mine."

Few people have the same level of spiritual maturity as my friend. Forgiveness is hard, especially when someone has caused you to question your worth and consider yourself unwanted. But the truth is that forgiveness alone can set you free from your bondage to the hurt the other person has caused you. Try to remember that those who intentionally hurt others are usually doing so to deal with their pain and frustrations. Then, even if you still don't "feel" like forgiving, decide to forgive anyway. Say out loud: "I forgive _____, whose words and/or actions have caused me great pain. Today, I am free from that pain, and I begin to move forward."

Forgiving someone does not excuse that person of responsibility for what was done to you, but it frees you of the heavy emotional burden of bitterness. The damage need not be permanent if you can manage to forgive, forget, and move forward.

It may not be necessary to break ties altogether with the person who hurt you, but I would advise taking some time apart so that you have a chance to heal fully.

WHEN REJECTION ARISES FROM WITHIN

So far, we have discussed the rejection we may encounter from our relationships and our circumstances—two areas over which we have little control. Each of us will experience mistreatment and rejection at some point in our lives. All of us will journey through difficult circumstances that may discourage us and cause us to doubt our worth. But what happens when the devaluation of ourselves doesn't come from other people or our external circumstances? What happens when we simply don't believe in ourselves? What do we do when we've rejected ourselves and denied our hearts a chance at dreaming?

According to the National Organization for Women, a nationwide study showed that 53 percent of thirteen-year-old girls aren't happy with their bodies. This figure increases to 78 percent for girls aged seventeen.[10] Studies also show that gender plays a vital role regarding the perception of intelligence, with women tending to believe themselves to be less intelligent than men.[11] This means that women are apt to underestimate their intelligence and abilities.

The feelings that detract from us don't always come from external elements. In many cases, they come from within. I have worked with many women who harbor harmful thoughts about

10. National Organization for Women, "Get the Facts: Body Image," https://now.org/now-foundation/love-your-body/love-your-body-whats-it-all-about/get-the-facts/.

11. Kerri Ann Renzulli, "Research finds women still get passed over for 'intellectual' jobs—but there's an easy way companies could fix that," CNBC.com, January 8, 2019, https://www.cnbc.com/2019/01/07/study-men-still-as-smarter-than-women-get-intellectual-jobs.html.

themselves without any prompting from insults uttered by others or from unfavorable circumstances surrounding them. These women insult themselves with thoughts that they would never dream of directing aloud at anyone else. The result of these thoughts is loneliness and a profound sense of disconnectedness. How many women disqualify themselves for promotion or sell themselves short of their dreams without the "help" of anyone else? How often is it that our negative thoughts and unhealthy self-image, rather than actual rejection by a person or an organization, hold us back?

Many women allow the experiences of their past to dictate the portrait of their future. One or two instances of failure or rejection become predictive of continued failure and rejection, leading some women to give up before they've even taken a chance. One woman told me that she knew that she would never find love again based on her husband's having divorced her. She assumed that every man she might meet would reject her just as her ex-husband had done. This type of erroneous thinking can turn into a self-fulfilling prophecy if we allow it to fester and grow in our minds.

> ONE SINGLE MISTAKE, ONE ISOLATED INSTANCE OF REJECTION, NEITHER EQUALS NOR INSTIGATES AN ENTIRE LIFE FULL OF ERRORS AND REJECTION.

The truth is that one single mistake, one isolated instance of rejection, neither equals nor instigates an entire life full of errors and rejection. It's easy enough for me to say that, and it may be simple enough for a woman to comprehend; but when an experience of failure or rejection utterly shakes a woman's world and leads her to label herself a failure, the matter of seeing the truth becomes quite complicated.

A sense of unworthiness is quickly compounded by additional mistakes and failures so that a woman's internal conversation takes a negative turn. Even if those around her are verbally affirming and encouraging, she is apt to tell herself, over and over again, "I'm so stupid"; "I'm a failure who can't succeed"; "Why would anybody love me?" For many women, silencing this negative self-talk is an impossibility. They aren't equipped to challenge these erroneous thoughts and temper their negativity with the truth, and so they unwittingly impose a limit on who they can be and what they can do, thereby stifling their full potential.

ALIGN YOUR THOUGHTS WITH YOUR WORTH

We must guard our minds and our thoughts, casting out untruths and "[taking] *captive every thought to make it obedient to Christ*" (2 Corinthians 10:5 NIV). Don't be one of those women who accept an incorrect definition of themselves and their worth based on past mistakes or current shortcomings. It is said that we are each our own worst critic. Let's cling to God's Word and commit to being our own best cheerleader!

And let's not put out a welcome mat for self-fulfilling prophecies of doom and gloom. On one occasion, I was driving away from a mall in Florida, and I thought to myself, "How terrible it would be if I were in an accident!" A few minutes later, another car crashed into my passenger door, and the driver fled the scene. Several years after that, I was making my way down a ladder and, with only four rungs to go, I thought, "If someone fell from here, it would be a hard fall!" Three seconds later, bam! I fell right to the floor. Some people look for prophecies, but, woman, you are the most accurate prophet over your own life. The conversation you keep up with yourself will largely determine your future. Ever since my auto accident and my fall from the ladder, I have been training myself to stop entertaining negative thoughts. Every time I receive a negative thought, I immediately say out loud (in spite of the strange looks this may earn from those around me), "I bind and paralyze all negative thoughts, in the name of Jesus." I then begin to confess the opposite of whatever it is that I thought, also out loud. This practice is powerful because you can't harbor two opposing thoughts simultaneously, and you can't think thoughts that are contrary to whatever you are speaking at a given moment.

If my mind says, "Omayra, you were wrong. How stupid of you. You always make the worst choices," then I say out loud, "Omayra, relax. Everything has a purpose in life. Maybe today, you don't see what you thought would happen, but later on, God will do something good with this. Trust Him. You did the best you could. You made a decision based on what you knew. You learned a great lesson that will serve you in the future. This will not happen again." With my confession, I stop the negative thoughts and unleash what I want to see in my future.

MONITOR YOUR SPEECH

I have spoken with countless women who frequently give voice to the negative views they have of themselves. Their words not only reflect their sense of inadequacy, low self-worth, and tendency toward self-deprecation; they reinforce those things, strengthening the barricade to success in life. Expecting only the worst and saying as much, these women essentially sentence themselves to a dissatisfying existence of mediocrity and discarded dreams.

Again, the key is bringing our thoughts into obedience to God—in other words, agreeing with what He says about us rather than what others may say or we may think—and being sure to speak only words that back up with these biblical truths about us. To make positive confessions that counteract any negative thoughts, we must develop a mental storage unit of scriptural truths. I'll get you started with the following truths and their scriptural sources, but I would highly recommend studying the Bible for yourself and mining it for the wonderful treasures it has for you.

WOMEN WHO EXPECT ONLY THE WORST AND SAY AS MUCH ESSENTIALLY SENTENCE THEMSELVES TO A DISSATISFYING EXISTENCE OF MEDIOCRITY AND DISCARDED DREAMS.

Because you are a daughter of the King of kings…

+ You are loved.

    I have loved you with an everlasting love; therefore with lovingkindness I have drawn you.   (Jeremiah 31:3)

+ Nothing can separate you from the love of God.

    Neither death nor life, nor angels nor principalities nor powers, nor things present nor things to come, nor height nor depth, nor any other created thing, shall be able to separate us from the love of God which is in Christ Jesus our Lord.   (Romans 8:38–39)

+ You can have confidence in Christ.

Blessed is the one who trusts in the LORD, whose confidence is in him.   (Jeremiah 17:7 NIV)

+ God will never fail you.

God is within her, she will not fall; God will help her at break of day.   (Psalm 46:5 NIV)

+ You are beautiful from the inside out.

Your beauty should not come from outward adornment, such as elaborate hairstyles and the wearing of gold jewelry or fine clothes. Rather, it should be that of your inner self, the unfading beauty of a gentle and quiet spirit, which is of great worth in God's sight.   (1 Peter 3:3–4 NIV)

+ All your needs will be met in the Lord.

My God shall supply all your need according to His riches in glory by Christ Jesus.   (Philippians 4:19)

GUARD YOUR GATES

Realize that your eyes and ears are the doors through which you gather the supply of thoughts you will have at your disposal. If you primarily watch shows and movies that depict the sufferings of a female protagonist at the hands of men, you are apt to develop a victim mentality and to think you're just as doomed as the women on TV. Suppose you gossip continually with your girlfriend about her disappointment with her spouse or significant other. In that case, you may develop an anti-male attitude that assumes the worst of every man you come across, and you may never give yourself the chance to find true love. Suppose all you read are the tabloids telling you of female celebrities' financial exploits and fashion wins. In that case, you may lose sight of your own goals and get caught up in chasing after fame, fortune, and fitness rather than building your character or investing in your education. Idolizing glamorous women with whom you really can't identify only alienates you further from your calling and may cause you to demean yourself because you feel you can't compete.

Everything that you receive through your senses stands a chance to be internalized as a thought, shaping the way you view yourself and your situation. How, then, can you guard your "gates" so that you receive only that which edifies you and spurs you on in the pursuit of your dreams?

Change what you see. Glory to God for the era of technology we now live in that allows us to access quality programming without being limited to the same demoralizing shows and movies. Glory to God for the rise of Christian music and movies full of faith and blessing. Many secular television programs and documentaries can likewise encourage us with stories of individuals who overcame the odds. Choose wisely what you watch, avoiding entertainment that does not edify or instruct. As you select quality shows and movies, your attitude will change for the better, and your confidence will soar.

Change what you say and hear. First Corinthians 15:33 wisely says, *"Do not be deceived: 'Evil company corrupts good habits.'"* Take care that in your conversations with other people, you avoid gossip and slander. If you do this, believe me when I tell you that your internal conversations will change. Years ago, I decided not to participate any longer in idle discussions, gossip, or negative conversations in general, such as those centered on complaining or venting frustrations. This decision has made a world of difference in my thought-life. If people are going to talk politics with me, they had better talk about the solutions they propose and not merely lament the problems we all know exist in our nations. The media does an excellent job laying out the issues without any help from us. Negative conversations rarely produce positive results.

> WHEN YOU AVOID GOSSIP AND
> SLANDER IN YOUR CONVERSATIONS
> WITH OTHER PEOPLE,
> YOUR INTERNAL CONVERSATIONS WILL
> CHANGE FOR THE BETTER.

If someone starts gossiping in my presence, I make an excuse and end the conversation. You can do the same. When I'm talking with friends, I like to be able to say at the end of our discourse, "Well, we've solved the world's problems, haven't we?" It is a joy to participate in productive conversations where you receive new ideas, gain a more positive perspective, and generate solutions. If necessary, update your circle of friends so that the content of your conversations adds value to your life rather than detracts from your joy.

Change what you read. Literature can be one of the most significant suppliers of thoughts. In addition to the Word of God, which is the most crucial text you can read, you should start seeking out works of literature that inspire, edify, and instruct—whether they are novels, nonfiction books, devotionals, journal articles, or something else. If you are already an avid reader, let nothing stop you from continuing with that habit. And if reading isn't among your habits, do what you can to make it one. Take advantage of the resources at your local library. If you struggle to find time to sit down and read, consider listening to an audiobook in your car or through earphones while exercising or going about your day. The words you ingest in this way can have a profound impact on your attitudes *and* your aptitudes.

PRACTICE HEALTHY SELF-TALK

When we adopt a demeaning attitude toward ourselves and chronically view ourselves negatively, we may begin blaming ourselves for problems outside our control. We may even increase our risk of mental health problems.[12] It can also set us up for failure because, in addition to the natural obstacles on the path to our goal, we also have to overcome our negative, doubting attitude. Wellness coach Elizabeth Scott writes, "One of the most obvious drawbacks about negative self-talk is that it's not positive. This sounds simplistic, but research has shown that positive self-talk is a greater predictor of success."[13]

Positive self-talk is essential to resist the damaging effects of rejection, whether it's directed at us by others or by ourselves. Some techniques that can orient your thoughts in a more positive direction include questioning your inner critic, replacing evil thoughts with good ones, and talking to yourself as you would speak to a treasured friend. If someone calls you ugly, look in the mirror and admire aloud some aspect of your appearance. If someone belittles you, remind yourself of your strengths and accomplishments. If someone excludes you from a gathering or a special event, remind yourself that the King of kings has called you His own and that you are *"accepted in the Beloved"* (Ephesians 1:6). Rise above rejection by remembering who you

---

12. Elizabeth Scott, MS, "The Toxic Effects of Negative Self-Talk," Verywell Mind online, February 25, 2020, https://www.verywellmind.com/negative-self-talk-and-how-it-affects-us-4161304.
13. Ibid.

are and *Whose* you are. No one can diminish the value of God's treasured daughter—a woman with a bright future of limitless potential.

Now, if you would only live like you believed that was true! In the next chapter, I'm going to teach you how to do just that.

Make sure that your projection faithfully represents what lies within—a confidence in your value because of the wonderful way you have been made, in the image of the One who created you.

Chapter 5

LIVE LIKE YOU'RE WORTH IT

Early on in pastoral ministry, a young woman in our church had the most beautiful singing voice you ever heard. She also wore the tightest-fitting, most revealing clothes you ever saw. As her pastor, I corrected her in love, not wanting to condemn her but only desiring that the image she presented in church be appropriate and befitting a godly young woman.

The young woman persisted in wearing scanty clothes, claiming that she wore the only clothes she had due to her family's limited financial resources. I purchased her some new, church-appropriate outfits, and yet she continued to come to the services wearing the old, revealing clothes.

One day, as I prayerfully meditated on the time, love, and patience I had invested in this young woman, I realized that the problem was not a shortage of financial resources. The problem rested in the emotional state of this young woman and the value she had assigned to herself. I saw that her wardrobe had been designed to earn admiration from men. This pretty, talented young woman was seeking praise from men for her looks to make up for the self-worth she lacked. In her mind, her beauty was synonymous with her value, and only if she turned heads and received looks of admiration did she consider herself worthy.

Once I reached this realization, I asked that she stop singing up front during our church services until she had come to understand who she was and how much she was worth. Sadly, this young woman refused to change her manner of dressing. She would not stop seeking through her appearance the approval and value she lacked at her core. It pains me to admit that she is now dealing with the consequences of failing to act on the loving advice of someone who only wanted what was best for her.

Countless women resort to the same methods to inflate their self-esteem. They debase themselves in their behavior and dress to get guys to notice them because they mistakenly base their value on the attention of the opposite sex. I have emphasized time and again to my four daughters, and I will never tire of doing so: by the way you dress, the way you speak, and the way you behave, you show the world whether you respect and value yourself. Many women devalue themselves in the eyes of others because they project a self that shows an utter lack of self-respect.

MANY WOMEN DEVALUE THEMSELVES IN THE EYES OF OTHERS BECAUSE THEY PROJECT A SELF THAT SHOWS AN UTTER LACK OF SELF-RESPECT.

Later on in this chapter, we will explore how specific elements of your wardrobe and your ways of speaking and behaving either enhance or detract from your value. But the first subject we will tackle is that of projection—the self you are presenting to the world.

HOW UPBRINGING AFFECTS PROJECTION

The way that we project ourselves has its roots in our upbringing. When our parents emphasize appearance, that attention tends to carry over into adulthood. In my household, there were four children—three girls and a boy—all born within six years of one another. Getting four young kids dressed and ready is no easy feat, yet my mother turned it into an art form. Not only were we flawlessly attired, but we were also taught to speak and behave impeccably. Wherever we went, people would comment on how well-dressed, well-spoken, and well-educated we were.

When we were very young, my mother would dress us one by one, from the oldest to the youngest. We would sit on the sofa, and we weren't allowed to move until all of us were ready to leave. My mother's theory was, if we left the sofa, we were bound to get dirty, wrinkle our perfectly ironed clothes, and mess up our hair, meaning she would have to start the process all over.

As we grew older and learned to dress ourselves, my mother would lay out our clothes on our beds. There on the mattress every morning was everything I was supposed to wear, from hair accessories down to my socks and coordinating shoes. If we were going to the beach that day, there would be a swimsuit, a pair of sandals, a beach towel, and even a little bag for me to carry along. If we were headed to church, there would be a dress, a dainty pair of shoes, and any coordinating accessories. If our day's plans included a park, there would be shorts, a matching shirt, and sneakers. Even if our mother hadn't told us where we were going on a given day, we could figure it out by looking at what she had laid out on the bed.

Before we left the house, her appraising eye scanned us from head to toe, and she would determine whether we had all prepared ourselves according to her preferences. My mother was never one to put up with chaos; she would never have dreamed of conjuring an excuse such as, "I have four kids; I can hardly get them all dressed, let alone make sure their outfits are coordinated." Her standards were unwavering when it came to cleanliness and presentability. She was always put together and perfumed, and we were expected to be the same.

For a while, my youngest sister had a slight speech impediment that made her say words out of order. My mother would correct her repeatedly, patiently, and lovingly, yet also with a rigidity that showed an unwillingness to allow any problem to impede my sister's development. Even though my mother also enlisted the help of a professional speech therapist, if my sister speaks without any imperfections today, it is because my mother didn't rest until the issue was fixed. I witnessed my mother teach my sister to think through what she wanted to say before speaking, open her mouth only when she was ready to say what she wished to express, and make her statement without stuttering and with all the words in the correct order. These were years of great patience and consistency.

As for my other siblings and me, a lack of speech impediments did not exempt us from lessons in diction, etiquette, and deportment. We were taught to speak with the appropriate tone of voice, according to what we were saying, and always in complete sentences. Vague terms like "that thing" weren't accepted. Everything had its name, and we had to use it accordingly.

Speaking all at once was prohibited; we learned to wait for our turn to talk, and we did so gladly, knowing we were guaranteed an equal opportunity to express ourselves. Interrupting was likewise disallowed, though we were given space to participate in "adult conversations" and share our opinion in an orderly, respectful way. We were also required to speak in complete sentences. We were to address adults as "sir" or "ma'am." Polite expressions such as "Excuse me," "Please," "Thank you," and "Good morning" were never forgotten. One look from our mother was all it took to let us know that we had failed to express ourselves correctly, and we were sure to rectify the problem immediately.

Laughter and good humor always filled our home, never any offensive jokes or derisive teasing. Screaming in the house was unacceptable (though it was permitted at the park). We were to knock on a door three times and then await a response before opening the door and entering. When we showed up somewhere, we were to greet everyone present—adults and children alike.

To this day, I still observe all these rules from my childhood. People will often say to me, "You can relax with me," to which I always laugh and answer the same: "No, I can't, because my mom would frown upon it." I thank God for giving me a mother who was intentional about teaching her children to take proper care of their appearance, self-expression, and conduct—to look, speak, and act with a sense of decorum and self-confidence that was evidence of how we valued ourselves. She knew that these three elements, adequately practiced, would open many doors for us. But if we slacked in our efforts, we would disqualify ourselves from countless opportunities.

I discovered very early on that my mother had been right about this. I see now that her diligent teaching was a key to my growing into the person I am today. I have taken care to pass her wisdom on to my daughters, and I pray they will do the same for their children someday.

WHAT MESSAGE ARE WE PROJECTING?

We just saw how my mother raised my siblings and me to dress, speak, and act in ways that showed respect to others and ourselves. The way we project ourselves to the world depends wholly on—and also reflects—the way we value ourselves. Let's explore the message we send with the clothes we wear, the words we speak (and the attitudes they express), and how we conduct ourselves.

THE CLOTHES WE WEAR

Today, I lay out my outfits as my mother did for me as a kid, arranging them on my bed or hanging them in the closet. My style tends to be a bit more formal than what is often required. For me, it isn't about "keeping up with appearances"; I feel more comfortable when I'm well-dressed. I'll confess that I sometimes feel overdressed, but I would rather be overdressed than underdressed.

Please understand me: dressing well does not in any way add to your value. You are worthy without dressy clothes. But dressing your best creates in you a sense of well-being and healthy self-satisfaction that improves your projection. I invite you to go to a luxurious store and try on a dress that you don't have the money to buy. This may seem materialistic, but please don't judge me for making this suggestion until you go and do it. Some would say, "No, that will bring me frustration!" Others will feel as if they are doing something useless or ridiculous. Let it bring you motivation; dare to do things that make you step out of your comfort zone.

Always try to look your best, whatever that means to you. Maybe you feel prettier when you put on a dress. Perhaps you feel more yourself in jeans and a flannel shirt. Either way, be thoughtful about coordinating your outfits. Comb your hair. Consider trying a new 'do. Spritz on some perfume, if you'd like. Apply some makeup.

> DRESSING WELL DOES NOT ADD TO YOUR VALUE, BUT DRESSING YOUR BEST CREATES IN YOU A SENSE OF WELL-BEING AND HEALTHY SELF-SATISFACTION THAT IMPROVES YOUR PROJECTION.

"But, wait!" you might be saying. "I don't know the first thing about makeup!" Many women avoid styling their hair or applying makeup because they feel they need special training to do these things. It isn't challenging to do a little research, whether online, in a recent magazine, or even as you're walking through the mall. Keep an eye out for women whose features are similar to yours, and imitate the colors and effects that appeal to you. I would never suggest attempting a look you aren't comfortable with or that doesn't complement your style. Pay attention to your age, body shape, and personality as you make any changes.

You don't have to spend a lot of money to look polished. There are probably some pieces already in your wardrobe or in a closet of someone you could borrow from that could make a big difference in your style. It's about being creative and getting the most out of what you already have.

Just as every woman is valuable, every woman is beautiful in her way. I think that with the proper science and a bit of creativity, you can project your best style without losing a pound, without undergoing an expensive surgery, and without feeling intimidated by the thinnest, most gorgeous models. How? It's effortless: you optimize all the elements that make up your physical appearance. In addition to your wardrobe, your eyes, your smile, and your overall demeanor contribute to your projection.

Some women rely on expensive surgeries and appearance-altering treatments to achieve the look they desire. Other women grow frustrated, thinking they will never look good enough because they can't afford a gym membership or a facelift. None of these alterations is necessary for improving your projection! With what you have, the way you are is more than enough for you to project your best "me" if you do it with the right attitude, within your resources, and, above all, with the confidence of knowing that you are valuable.

THE WORDS WE SPEAK (AND THE ATTITUDES THEY EXPRESS)

Few people fully understand the power of their words. Again, it says in Proverbs 18:21, *"Death and life are in the power of the tongue."* There is great debate over the relationship between our words and our attitudes. Some people contend that our words determine the way we feel, while others believe that our feelings determine what we say. Do you speak positively because you have a positive attitude? Or do you have a positive attitude because you speak positively? I believe the two are linked cyclically, affecting each other in turn. The influence goes in both directions. There are days when you feel awesome, and you'll express yourself accordingly. There are other days when you feel bad, but if you express yourself as if you were feeling awesome, you'll begin to feel better.

SPEAK UP

Thanks in large part to my mother, I've always been good with words. I've never been shy when addressing anyone in any context. As kids, whenever my siblings and I were in a position of having a request to make of our parents, I was sent to make our case. I was always happy to oblige and usually returned to my siblings with the permission granted.

I understand the emotional charge that words receive and project. Still, I can't help emphasizing the importance of speaking out, especially for a gender that has been silenced for so many generations. Not every woman is good with words or feels comfortable expressing herself. If daring to speak up is not something that comes naturally to us, we must conquer our fear and determine to talk, especially if it means exposing a wrong done to a vulnerable population or ourselves.

The spread of the #MeToo movement in 2017, with thousands of women across the world publicly breaking their silence about sexual harassment and abuse they had suffered, brought a sense of empowerment to many who had long felt invisible in their victimization. Anyone who has been sexually abused or molested should not remain silent but should notify a trusted authority figure who can offer protection and guidance as they advance forward.

Many women also suppress rather than express their feelings of frustration, offense, anger, and embarrassment, either because they feel that women are not supposed to speak up or because they have been made to doubt the validity of their feelings. Don't let yourself be a victim of abuse or gaslighting. Don't stay silent about your pain or your other emotions. When you speak up and share what's on your heart and mind with a trusted friend or counselor—someone who will listen with compassion and affirm your value—you will find the relief and freedom your soul needs. You are free to tell your story, and, woman, it's a story worth telling.

KNOW WHAT YOU WANT, AND SAY WHAT YOU MEAN

Some women haven't learned to speak clearly and express precisely what they want or expect. A man recently related to me his frustration with his girlfriend because of her habit of saying one thing while meaning just the opposite. For example, she might tell him, "You don't have to come see me," and then, when he didn't come, she'd say: "Actually, I did want you to come see me." Many women play this game, purposefully expressing the opposite of what they want or need. Other women can't make up their minds, and because they aren't able to identify their wants and needs, they can't express them consistently.

My husband likes to talk about the "big fights" we used to have—our arguments over where we should eat or what we should cook for dinner. Do those ever happen in your household? Well, we finally put an end to them. I decided some time ago that if my husband asked for my opinion on something, I would tell him exactly what I wanted. No more "Whatever you want, dear"! If someone asks to know your preference, then say it honestly and in detail. Problem solved! A man will get frustrated if he's sitting in a steakhouse with his wife, knowing she wants Asian food—and that she'll eventually get mad because she's stuck eating steak. You aren't rude if the other person asks what you want to do or where you want to go.

Who can respect your desires, feelings, and preferences if you won't dare to express them? Deferring continually to other people will eventually lead you to devalue yourself—and for others to devalue you, as well. I understand that women sometimes can't identify how they're feeling. But that is an exception to the norm. Let's work on mustering the courage and self-confidence to speak up! The ability to express ourselves clearly and confidently is of utmost importance in the quest to value ourselves and to earn the respect of others. Believe me when I say that there is someone out there who cares about what you have to say and will listen to you. If you remain quiet and continually demure, you demonstrate a failure to value yourself and your views.

IF SOMEONE ASKS TO KNOW YOUR PREFERENCE, THEN SAY IT HONESTLY AND IN DETAIL.

THINK BEFORE SPEAKING

While we're summoning the confidence to speak up, we can't afford to forget the importance of weighing our words before giving them a voice. Blurting out the first thing that comes to mind is never a wise thing to do! I can't abide women who shrug their shoulders and say, matter-of-factly, "I say it like it is"; "I don't beat around the bush." Speaking impulsively without forethought rarely produces good results.

The book of Proverbs in the Bible is full of Scriptures that back me up on this point. Let me share just a few of them.

Those who guard their lips preserve their lives, but those who speak rashly will come to ruin. (Proverbs 13:3 NIV)

The one who has knowledge uses words with restraint, and whoever has understanding is even-tempered.
(Proverbs 17:27 NIV)

Those who guard their mouths and their tongues keep themselves from calamity. (Proverbs 21:23 NIV)

Do you see someone who speaks in haste? There is more hope for a fool than for them. (Proverbs 29:20 NIV)

Even fools are thought wise if they keep silent, and discerning if they hold their tongues. (Proverbs 17:28 NIV)

I don't know about you, but I want to be perceived as wise, knowledgeable, understanding, and even-tempered. I don't want to be the fool described in those verses!

More than a decade ago at a pastors' meeting, my husband made a masterful illustration on this same topic using the words of the apostle Paul in 1 Corinthians 13:11: *"When I was a child, I spoke as a child, I understood as a child, I thought as a child; but when I became a man, I put away childish things."* Children tend to speak first, think second, and meditate last. That's the way their immature minds work. Young people say what they feel without any forethought or premeditation. Let's not be childish in our communication! We need to think before speaking and, when we open our mouths, to make our words *"full of grace, seasoned with salt, so that* [we] *may know how to answer everyone"* (Colossians 4:6 NIV).

Wise women don't go around saying everything they feel to whomever they see. That would be a display of childish, immature behavior. We must make sure to meditate first, asking ourselves, "What message do I want to convey? And how can I best communicate that message without offending my listener?" Now, don't make the mistake of meditating too much or overthinking the message to the point where you forfeit your chance to talk. Your message is essential, and, again, someone will want to listen! Just be sure to weigh your words before uttering them.

THE WAY WE CONDUCT OURSELVES

I remember overhearing some of my uncles planning an outing for themselves and some of the boys in the family. As they were discussing who would get to go along, one of my uncles said, "If all the children were like Lucy's [my mother's children—in other words, my siblings and me], I would take them, but so and so's kids don't know how to behave, so they can't come." I'm sure that some of my cousins, had they overheard this conversation, would have called my uncle's assessment unfair. But the fact remains that their habitually poor behavior became why they were excluded from a family outing. The way we conduct ourselves is one means by which others measure our character. Many people have lost out on far bigger privileges and opportunities than family outings due to poor behavior.

EXTEND COMMON COURTESY

Good manners never go out of style, even though the definition of "good manners" changes slightly over time and according to shifts in our culture. Behavior that was once appropriate and even expected a hundred years ago, such as a man kissing the hand of a woman in greeting, might be considered inappropriate today—and might even be grounds for a legal suit over sexual harassment. Yet, universal principles of proper behavior do not cease to exist for specific contexts, such as the workplace, houses of worship, educational institutions, government buildings, and even stores and restaurants. We should observe the basic principles of common courtesy and treat others with dignity and respect.

My husband and daughters like to tease me about my emphasis on (or my "obsession with") propriety, suggesting that it's over-the-top. My husband will roll his eyes and mutter sarcastically, "You and your protocols." Yet he frequently consults me on the proper protocol when meeting with certain people or visiting unusual places where he isn't sure what is expected of him. On the one hand, he chafes under my "protocols," and on the other hand, he knows he needs them. That's the way it goes with good manners. Some of them may seem burdensome or excessive, but they go a long way in promoting order and harmonious coexistence with others.

> PROPER MANNERS AREN'T JUST
> ABOUT SHOWING RESPECT TO OTHERS.
> THEY'RE ABOUT RESPECTING YOURSELF.

Commitment to punctuality, addressing those in positions of authority with respect, conducting ourselves with propriety in public and in private—all of these behaviors bring rewards and communicate our value. Just as with our clothing and our speech, good manners don't increase our value, but they indicate to others that we value ourselves, making them inclined to do the same. Proper manners promote a healthy coexistence with others and also affirm our value. It isn't just about showing respect to others. It's about respecting yourself.

EVALUATE YOUR MANNERS

Are you "obsessed" with good manners like I am? If so, you can first thank God for whoever it was that taught you the importance of proper conduct. Second, you can stop yourself from looking down on anyone as inferior for having less refined manners. Not everyone is blessed to be raised by someone who instills godly values in them and teaches them how to interact with others. Help and teach those who need it, as much as you can, without degrading them or making them feel bad.

If, on the other hand, you feel a pang of conviction over a lack of manners, don't feel bad without doing anything about it. Maybe you need to brush up on common courtesies or make a closer study of some of the hallmarks of behavioral protocols in a professional setting, such as your workplace. Practice projecting courtesy, being considerate of others, and treating everyone you meet with dignity and respect.

IT STARTS WITH SELF-RESPECT AND AUTHENTICITY

Our dress, words, and behavior don't define us, but they make a strong statement about our self-perception and the value we place on ourselves. I learned this truth from a young age because my mother taught me to dress in a way that projects someone who respects her body; to express my thoughts, beliefs, and desires in a way that projects someone who values her mind; and to act in a manner that projects someone who respects herself and others, thereby opening doors of opportunity left and right.

The young woman whose story I shared at the start of this chapter was raised by a mother brought up in a church of strict religiosity that dictated what people wore and how they wore it. Not wanting her daughter to be subject to such stringent rules, she granted her complete freedom in selecting her wardrobe. And this freedom led to the daughter seeking attention and admiration from men through her clothing choices. Her mother had tried teaching her not to put too much emphasis on the praise of men, but she failed to make her daughter understand the true source of her worth. As a result, earning the admiration of men became the daughter's primary goal, and her attire became the primary method of achieving it. Her mother gave her daughter the freedom she never had, without giving her the ability to value herself for who she was rather than how she looked and project herself accordingly.

Some people try to project what they are not. They may be emotionally damaged and distraught on the inside, but they paste on a smile and project an appearance of perfect happiness to the world. They may project an attitude of kindness and concern to mask a hidden agenda or ulterior motive with less-than-kind intentions. But a divided life such as this is hard work to keep up. Plus, they are bound to be found out at some point. Jesus addressed this fact when He said to a group of Pharisees, *"A tree is recognized by its fruit....How can you who are evil say anything good? For the mouth speaks what the heart is full of"* (Matthew 12:33, 34 NIV). In spite of any efforts we may make to project a false or altered identity, our true personalities will ultimately shine through, accurately reflecting the value we place on ourselves.

Our wardrobes, our words, and our way of behaving are important elements of our projection, reflecting to the world what lies within us and how we feel about it. We need to make sure that our projection faithfully represents what lies within us—confidence in our value because of the wonderful way we have been made, in the image of the One who created us. Let's not cheapen or devalue ourselves by compromising our dress, keeping silent when we have something to say, or behaving rudely or with selfish intentions. When we dress modestly, speak thoughtfully, and treat others with courtesy and respect, we project the value we know we have.

When you value yourself properly,

something is activated within you

that pushes you forward,

ignites your passion, and propels

you to become the vibrant woman

you want to be.

Chapter 6

PASSIVE WISHING VS. ACTIVE DREAMING

There was a little girl who felt dissatisfied with her life. Nothing seemed good enough or fun enough for her. One day, a sorceress approached the girl and told her she would fulfill one of her wishes. The girl was delighted at first, but then she began to fret over which wish to choose. She had so many hopes that were important to her that it was impossible to choose only one. Seeking to teach her a valuable lesson, the sorceress told her that she would grant her one wish each day until the girl was satisfied.

The girl was ecstatic, believing all her dreams would come true, one after another. From that point on, the girl went to the sorceress every morning with joy and enthusiasm. Day after day, a new dream came true, and she believed herself to be moving closer to complete happiness. Weeks passed, and it wasn't long before the girl realized that the fulfillment of her wishes had not brought her the joy and happiness she had hoped for at first. The realization of many of her requests caused her disappointment and even pain. Almost every dream was the whim of an empty little girl. She received the toys she had longed for and the possessions she'd always dreamed of, but they were not what she had expected. The girl grew sadder and sadder as the fulfillment of her wishes failed to make her happy. Soon she began to fear the fulfillment of her dreams.

One day, the disappointment she felt was so great that she went to the sorceress and told her that she no longer wanted to receive a daily wish. She was afraid of living, fearful of waking up every day awaiting the fulfillment of another desire. She tearfully asked the sorceress to fulfill only one of her dreams: the dream to live as she had lived before when she enjoyed life.

The charming sorceress took pity on the girl, waved her magic wand, and disappeared. The girl ran home. She was happy because she knew that now she would diligently seek her great dream rather than waste time on trivial, short-term whims.

IT IS THE PROCESS OF WORKING TOWARD AND ACHIEVING OUR DREAMS THAT ENRICHES US AND MAKES US HAPPY.

We tend to think, "If only all my dreams would come true, then I would be truly happy." Yet it is the process of working toward and achieving our dreams that enriches us and makes us happy. Having our desires fulfilled automatically as if by magic does not bring half the satisfaction of working diligently to achieve the desired end and finally, through hard work and determination, bringing that end to fruition.

DREAMS DEMAND DEVOTION AND EFFORT

Joel Osteen tweeted a phrase that I find pretty profound: "The difference between a dream and a wish is that a wish is something you just hope happens, but a dream you put actions behind. The scripture says, 'Faith without works is dead.' Wishing is not going to get you anywhere."[14]

An article recapping a commencement address delivered by singer-songwriter Dolly Parton captures the same message:

"Do not confuse dreams with wishes," [Parton] said at one point to the 12,000-strong crowd. "There is a difference. Dreams are where you visualize yourself being successful at what's important for you to accomplish. Dreams build convictions because you work hard to pay the price to make sure that they come true. Wishes are hoping good things will happen to you, but there's no fire in your gut that causes you to put everything forth to overcome all the obstacles. So you have to dream more," Parton added, "and never, ever, ever blame somebody else if it doesn't happen."[15]

People often use the terms *wish*, *goal*, and *dream* interchangeably. However, there are nuanced differences among the three.

---

14. Joel Osteen, Twitter post, September 6, 2019, 9:55 a.m., https://twitter.com/joelosteen/status/1169972271349469184?lang=eng.

15. Annie Zaleski, "11 Years Ago: Dolly Parton Gives UT Knoxville Commencement Address, Earns Honorary Doctorate," TheBoot.com, May 8, 2020, https://www.theboot.com/dolly-parton-ut-knoxville-commencement-address-2009/.

WHAT IS A WISH?

One dictionary defines *wish* as "a desire for something to happen or be done: a feeling of wanting to do or have something; an act of thinking about something that you want and hoping that you will get it or that it will happen in some magical way."[16] Desiring is intrinsic to human nature and one of the fundamental mechanisms driving human behavior.

Wanting things is normal. If you are hungry, you want food. If you are sleepy, you want to rest. Wishes can be about enjoying the fulfillment of legitimate needs, such as shelter, sustenance, security, and the like. Wishes are not necessarily pure or without ulterior motive, however. Wayward human nature may prompt us to wish for something out of jealousy, lust, dissatisfaction driven by comparison, or another sinful source.

> WISHES CAN BE ABOUT ENJOYING THE FULFILLMENT OF LEGITIMATE NEEDS, BUT THEY ARE NOT NECESSARILY PURE OR WITHOUT ULTERIOR MOTIVE.

Wishes are also easily influenced by the achievements and possessions of those around us. For example, let's say a friend of yours buys a brand-new house. You may suddenly feel dissatisfied with your own home and wish for a bigger, newer, better abode. Or maybe someone you know is always trading in her car for the latest model with all the bells and whistles. You've been satisfied with your car, but now you wish you could upgrade for

16. *Merriam-Webster's English Language Learner's Dictionary Online*, s.v. "wish," accessed May 10, 2021, https://www.learnersdictionary.com/definition/wish.

no other reason than your friend is always doing just that. It is all too easy to have our wishes dictated by somebody else.

You cannot afford to let someone else establish your desires for you. Your desires must be your own, not those of your spouse, boss, friend, child, or anyone else. They are yours, and you must own them, or you will not execute them. There is no energy in other people's goals. There is only energy in what is within you.[17] That's why we don't feel any better when our "wishes are granted"—when we receive what we've been hoping for, whether it's a house, a car, a job, a marriage, a business, or something else—if the desire for that item or that achievement didn't originate within ourselves.

WHAT IS A GOAL?

By definition, a *goal* is "the end toward which effort is directed: aim." Goals are specific objectives that you are focused on achieving, and they spell out the details of what you have envisioned or imagined. Goals are made more reachable when we write them down and develop a corresponding action plan that lays out a timetable to complete them. In this way, a goal is a dream with an assigned deadline. According to Dave Ramsey, the goals that we hope to achieve must be specific, measurable, personal, assigned a time limit, and written down.[18]

Goals, when pushed to the back burner and left unpursued, turn into wishes. This reversal often happens at the start of a new year, when people are fueled with fresh energy over their New Year's resolutions. Yet these "resolutions" that people draw up often amount to wishes that are never within reach because of a failure to commit and do the work. Countless people, men and

---

17. See Ramsey Solutions, "The Keys To Achieving Your Goals," July 17, 2020, https://www.daveramsey.com/blog/the-keys-to-achieving-your-goals.
18. Ibid.

women alike, resolve to exercise and attain a healthier lifestyle. They enroll at a gym or purchase expensive workout equipment for their home. Within a few weeks, however, a large proportion of these people are no longer going to the gym or making time to exercise. Their "resolution" was an empty wish to be fit and healthy, not a commitment to achieve that end.

Likewise, many women want to eat healthier, go to church regularly, or study a particular discipline. Unless these goals are acted upon, they remain as mere wishes. Only when our goals are accompanied by a plan and by a serious commitment do we manage to achieve them.

WHAT IS A DREAM?

Dreams are more complex than wishes and goals. Our dreams tend to be the product of our imagination—a picture of how we hope our future will look. And clearly defining our dreams can be the difference between simply surviving and truly thriving. Just as a goal without commitment is only a wish, a dream without a corresponding set of goals is nothing more than a detailed wish.

Wishing and desiring are passive; dreaming is active. Dreams generally motivate us to act, laying out the steps we must take and providing us with the mindset and drive to go the distance and achieve what we want. A dream defines our purpose and serves as a key focal point for our life, marking out the place we plan to be in the future.

A DREAM DEFINES OUR PURPOSE AND SERVES AS A KEY FOCAL POINT FOR OUR LIFE, MARKING OUT THE PLACE WE PLAN TO BE IN THE FUTURE.

As young girls and later as teenagers, most of us probably had dreams of our future selves and the type of life we would lead. Over time, we may have clung to one or more of these dreams, or maybe we discarded them altogether and generated an entirely new set as we aged. In shaping our dreams, we must reach within to discover what we long to do, who we want to be, and what we are willing to commit to—physically, emotionally, and spiritually. In the next chapter, we will look more closely at the process of developing our dreams. Sometimes, this process will require us to learn new things and master new skills. Ideally, the fact that we are working toward fulfilling a dream should make this process more pleasant than painful. When we focus on our desired destiny, we can muscle through and "enjoy the journey."

Dreams serve as guides because old dreams can speak to the heart of who we are today. Dreams don't have to be specific careers or achievements; they can be anything that brings us joy and satisfaction. Again, as we grow and mature, we are constantly restructuring and redefining our personal goals. Failing to restructure our dreams to accommodate our present circumstances can be a severe mistake. The creativity required for monitoring the progress we make toward our dream is a lifelong process that can express itself in different forms during the various phases of our life. The specifics of our dreams may change over time, but if we study them closely and compare them with our childhood wishes, we are likely to notice some strands of similarity.

VULNERABILITY LEADS TO VISION

For some years now, I have conducted a morning show on our radio station. During a recent broadcast, I had to do something I never do—something I will never do again. The reason?

I don't sing. Period. I don't even sing in the shower. I have no musical talent whatsoever. When I was in sixth grade, I was kicked out of a children's choir because the director said—in front of everyone, I might add—that I was causing all the other kids to sing out of tune. The humiliation of this experience still stings. And on this particular day, out of nowhere, all the other radio-show hosts committed to singing live and letting their listeners vote for who they thought sounded best. Going in, I knew my chances of winning were zero.

Now, why did I agree to sing on the radio? (By the way, it was horrible. I can't even listen to the recording.) One reason I agreed is that I knew that making yourself vulnerable and tackling uncomfortable situations is one way to grow your character. Vulnerability isn't weakness. It's the emotional risk of exposing yourself to something uncomfortable. When it was my turn to sing, I sincerely wanted to cry and run away. But when I did it, even though I sang horribly, I felt that I was being made braver because I dared to do something I had never done, even knowing that I wasn't going to do it well. Vulnerability can give you a chance to learn something new about yourself.

When I dared to sing on the radio, I confirmed something important: not only is singing not among my talents, it isn't something I desire to do—not because I do it poorly, but because of a simple lack of interest in singing. By singing in a public setting and exposing a vulnerable part of me, I confirmed that singing is not something I desire to improve at because I just don't like doing it. Making discoveries such as this can help us identify more clearly the things we do desire to do and pursue.

I may have no interest in or talent for singing. Still, I want to contribute to the morning radio program—cheering up our listeners, connecting with them, and motivating them to take positive action. That's another reason I dared to sing on that fateful morning. Because I recognized my value as a resource on the radio program, I mustered the courage to do something I neither wanted to do nor was good at doing. I transcended my comfort zone and made myself vulnerable to bless others.

DREAMING STARTS WITH RECOGNIZING OUR STRENGTHS AND ACCEPTING OUR VULNERABILITIES

My area of vulnerability—a lack of vocal talent—may seem like a trivial matter. But the truth is that any area of weakness can create a raw place in our soul where we experience shame, humiliation, and hurt. In some cases, a weakness might be the result of a poor decision or a grave mistake. If that is true for you, you'll need to forgive yourself to find healing in that area. If you're going to value yourself in a way that propels you to pursue your dreams, you can't go on feeling upset with yourself for stumbling over the same stone twice or for having trusted the wrong person. Reflect on your past experiences, recognize the pain that resulted, and release it. Then keep moving forward and becoming the person you want to be.

There are three critical things that every woman who values herself has to learn to live with to accept and fully love herself. If we are to live with dignity, we must accept the elements beyond our ability to change from one day to the next. Self-acceptance is a necessary practice for becoming the people we want to be. Rather than dwelling on what we can't do or don't have, we celebrate our strengths while acknowledging those areas of weakness that we probably won't change (such as an utter lack of musical skill). Only by understanding our present situation in these three areas can we assess who we are and where we are, then take steps to become who we want to be and do what we want to do. Of these three areas, the second is the only one that you are powerless to change, and that is your age. You can experience transformation in the other two areas as you become the woman you want to be, but not until you have recognized and accepted them as they are currently.

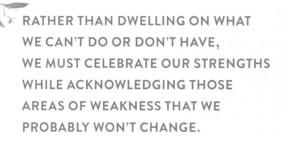

RATHER THAN DWELLING ON WHAT WE CAN'T DO OR DON'T HAVE, WE MUST CELEBRATE OUR STRENGTHS WHILE ACKNOWLEDGING THOSE AREAS OF WEAKNESS THAT WE PROBABLY WON'T CHANGE.

ACCEPT YOUR PHYSICAL APPEARANCE

So many women focus almost exclusively on their external features, praising themselves for their virtues and doing everything within their power and budget to root out imperfections. Yet even the most picture-perfect model is bound to find some flaw with her appearance. As they say, "You always want what you don't have." Tall women would prefer to be short. Curvier women would rather be slender; slender women wouldn't mind some curves. Women with poker-straight hair wish for curls, while curly-haired women try every method under the sun for straightening their ringlets. Reaching a place of being satisfied with our appearance is important because it frees up time and energy for what matters in the long run.

A woman gave a testimony in our church after being freed of one of her biggest fears. She explained that she had never worn skirts because of the way her family would mock her for her skinny legs. But she decided to participate in a "dress day" some other pastors and I had organized to celebrate our femininity. At the age of fifty, she put on a skirt for the first time in her life and showed her legs. As she did this, something broke inside her. She received many compliments from people who remarked admiringly just how different she looked, but I don't think it was because of the skirt. I think it was because she had finally accepted herself as she was, without feeling the need to hide or conceal what had previously been a source of shame.

Right now, I want you to go take a look in the mirror and say to yourself, "This is who I am." Take in your height, weight, and physical features. Trust me, you have everything you need to be what you want to be. I'll tell you something else: I am 100 percent certain that there is something in your physique that some other woman wishes she had. It's always that way.

ACCEPT YOUR AGE

We live in a culture that's obsessed with youthfulness. I admit I've been guilty of this obsession, making use of antiaging face creams and taking care of myself in any way that will help me look as youthful as possible. People will often say, for example, "Your forties are the new twenties," intending to bolster self-esteem and encourage adults that they can have as much vitality, strength, and attractive looks in their later years as they did in the prime of their youth.

I can buy those ideas for a little while, but, at the same time, I want to act and dress my actual age because doing so preserves my dignity and expresses my value. I don't want to be twenty; I want to be my age, whether it's forty or eighty. I want to possess and be respected for the wisdom of my age, not be looked down upon for the ignorance and inexperience that I had in my twenties.

Moreover, having two daughters in their twenties right now, I can tell you that it brings me more honor to see myself as their mother and not as if I were equal to them. That's acceptance of one's age, and it's a necessary step if we are to make the most of where we are in our life's journey.

ACCEPT YOUR CIRCUMSTANCES

When I talk about circumstances, I refer to the geographic, economic, and political culture in which you live. Except for certain situations—for example, someone fulfilling a prison sentence—your circumstances can be altered, and it may be that a change in circumstances will help immensely in your quest to become the person you are meant to be. But, as I said, it isn't always possible to change your circumstances; even if you can relocate, you must first acknowledge and accept your starting point.

I live in Puerto Rico, a small island in the Caribbean. Here, the phenomenon of six degrees of separation is reduced to probably two or three degrees, maximum. This sense of connectedness, of being widely known, causes many people to adopt a false sense of greatness. Even the smallest of fish feels like a whale in this tiny fishbowl. And in the world of sports, for example, we have a weekly battle for the so-called "Universal Title of Wrestling"—imagine, the world's best wrestler, decided not in a massive arena in a major city but in a small court in a humble Puerto Rican municipality such as Caguas or Bayamón. I may be poking fun, but I think this is an excellent example of a lack of acceptance of one's geography.

In the same way, your present economic situation must be taken into account. If you've been fiscally responsible, making sound financial decisions, living without debt, and cushioning your savings account regularly, I commend you. But that doesn't describe the financial standing of the majority of women. Many women live beyond their means, wanting to appear to have what they don't—and accruing loads of debt in the process. I learned a long time ago that having a debt problem results from wanting to have what you have not worked for yet. Strive for what you want, work hard—there isn't anything wrong with that. Just be sure that your income can support your lifestyle, or you will find yourself up to your neck in bills and other outstanding debts, and the fulfillment of your dreams will be farther away than ever.

As for our political culture, every nation has certain indigenous beliefs passed down from generations before that shape the political environment in which we live. These beliefs often contain underpinnings of gender bias, and we women would do well to be aware of them. Part of your culture may sanction a mindset that you will need to challenge and possibly strive to change to maintain your value. In Latin American countries, for example, women face the strong forces of machismo and feminism. Every Latin American woman must acknowledge the impact of both these ideals on both her culture and her convictions if she is to value herself properly and pursue her dreams in earnest.

When we acknowledge and accept our circumstances, we enable ourselves to assess them with greater objectivity and live without regrets, even as we look forward to a better future. Don't dwell on what is or what "can't" be, but look around and give yourself courage today, now, just as you are. Understand that this is the only way you can be everything you want to be. As you accept and recognize your geographic, economic, and political situation, be intentional about showing yourself love and grace. Why wait for someone else to do this when you can do it for yourself? We are constantly seeking the approval of others when the approval that matters the most must come from ourselves. Too many people wait for that proverbial pat on the back. Pat yourself on the back!

From this exercise of recognition and acceptance, you can move on to define what you want to do and the person you want to be. You may discover that you have been living on autopilot, as it were, going through the motions without giving much thought to where you are and where you are headed. But when you are a woman who highly values herself, you unleash what some psychologists call "activation energy."

[Activation energy] is actually a term used by chemists to describe the minimum amount of energy required to initiate a chemical reaction, but it's been adapted by psychologists to describe the motivation required to begin a task. When there are too many hurdles in place, and when our motivation isn't sufficient to overcome those hurdles, we'll choose something easier to do.[19]

Activation energy is that force that makes you get up early in the morning to pray when your body would rather stay in bed. Activation energy is what gets you to the gym to exercise even when you know your entire body will be sore the next day. Activation energy is what empowers you to put the chocolate cake aside when you want to devour it.

When you value yourself properly, something is activated within you that pushes you forward, ignites your passion, and

19. Jaime L. Kurtz, PhD, "Activation Energy: How It Keeps Happiness at a Distance," *Psychology Today*, July 10, 2016, https://www.psychologytoday.com/us/blog/happy-trails/201607/activation-energy-how-it-keeps-happiness-distance.

propels you to become the vibrant woman you want to be. Not sure yet who that woman is? Undecided as to what you dream of doing? Then read on!

Your dreams

must be authentic—

yours and no one else's.

DISCOVER THE DREAM WITHIN

𝓢ome childhood yearnings are never dropped, hence the term "lifelong dreams." Yet, other dreams will change dramatically or even be discarded throughout our lives. What did you dream of being or doing as a child? What feedback did you get about those dreams from the people closest to you—your parents, teachers, and friends? Have you achieved any of those childhood dreams, or did they all change as you grew into adulthood? What are your dreams today, and what are you doing to make them happen?

Maybe you have struggled to convert your dreams into realities. Or perhaps, like many women, you've forgotten how to dream in the first place. The process of dreaming revolves around answering four essential questions: what, why, when, and how.

1. What do you want to achieve?

2. Why do you want to achieve it?

3. When do you want to achieve it?

4. How will you achieve it?

One definition of a *dream* is "something that you have wanted to very much to do, be, or have for a long time."[20]. A great dream, then, is an intense desire or aspiration for something that, if achieved, would fulfill or satisfy an inner longing or desire (at least, we believe it will). A big dream is a powerful idea.

Each of us probably has a secret list—or maybe it's a not-so-secret list—of things we want in life. Those desires are transformed into dreams when they go beyond pure longings and become our focus, our engine. A dream can be something as simple as wanting to be a better person, wanting to make a difference in the lives of others, securing a job, earning a college degree, buying a car, or building a house.

A great dream is a bold vision of the future, a concept that scares and excites you at the same time. Carefully choose what is important to you so that you may have a vision that is bright and clear. Don't be afraid to go against the grain and avoid the "follow-the-crowd" mentality. You don't necessarily need to fit in with your peers to achieve your dreams. Many people who dreamed great dreams and found the joy of fulfilling those dreams were long considered at odds with the world around them—pioneers in their field or even pariahs in their society.

Just think of Susan Boyle, a Scottish woman who, at forty-seven years of age, took an unexpected leap to fame when she claimed the second-place prize in the third season of *Britain's Got*

---

20. *Merriam-Webster's English Learner's Dictionary Online*, s.v. "dream," accessed May 10, 2021, https://www.learnersdictionary.com/definition/dream.

Talent and went on to record an album that topped the Billboard charts in November 2009, becoming the second-best-selling album of that year with over 3.1 million copies sold. The unlikely star—a woman who had grown up the victim of teasing and intimidation, having suffered brain damage at birth, and had struggled with learning disabilities at school and eventually been diagnosed with Asperger's syndrome—had been rejected time and again by other vocal competitions. Unfazed by this repeated rejection, she auditioned for *Britain's Got Talent* to honor the memory of her late mother, who had been an avid fan of the show. The audience and judges were skeptical about her ambitions since her stage presence hardly seemed to be that of a rising vocal star. Yet from the first notes of the song "I Dreamed a Dream," she blew away all who listened and abruptly overturned their doubts. Three years later, a stage musical based on the life of Susan Boyle toured the United Kingdom, with Boyle herself making cameo appearances.[21] Talk about persevering in the pursuit of a great dream!

A GREAT DREAM IS A BOLD VISION OF THE FUTURE, A CONCEPT THAT SCARES AND EXCITES YOU AT THE SAME TIME.

Most women probably don't have such lofty dreams for themselves as stardom. Some of the more traditional dreams of women include getting married, having children, getting promoted, developing healthy friendships, and keeping a beautiful home. Yet even these are worthy goals, as long as we aren't stifling any aspirations that others have deemed unreachable, such as competing at the Olympics (and maybe

21. Jeannette L. Nolen, "Susan Boyle," *Britannica*, April 20, 2020, https://www.britannica.com/biography/Susan-Boyle.

even winning a gold medal), traveling the world, or walking on the moon. Start thinking—and take the limits off. What are your dreams?

GETTING READY TO GO AFTER GREAT DREAMS

When I analyze my dreams, I see that they are the product of my life experiences—of the things that, at some point, awakened a passion within me. And that is what your dreams must be made of if you are to see them fulfilled. They must be the product of you seeing beyond the present moment and mentally shaping the path that you must travel to reach them. Your dreams must be the product of your desires, mixed with your decisions, molded according to the direction you will take to achieve them.

In the words of Dave Ramsey:

> All goals begin with a dream. Now it's good to have a dream, but I meet a lot of people who have been praying about their dream for 20 years and have done nothing about it. Everybody has a great idea. But people who put their great ideas to work are the ones who end up being millionaires.[22]

Many women don't have clear goals, either short-term or long-term. It's not that they don't think about their future; they do so vaguely, feeling that they can't do anything in the present to achieve their future goals. Our dreams should give us a reason for getting out of bed in the morning, acting as a compass for our days and providing us with a sense of purpose and direction. However, because of an inward orientation and a

22. "Dave Ramsey: Put Your Dreams to Work to Build Wealth," *Success*, December 18, 2009, https://www.success.com/dave-ramsey-put-your-dreams-to-work-to-build-wealth/.

tendency to focus on the needs of others, such as their families and friends, many women don't dream beyond finishing their studies, securing a job, marrying, and starting a family. Many women don't dream past today because they have become too caught up in their myriad roles and responsibilities, which we discussed in an earlier chapter.

How about you? Are you, today, in the place where you dreamed you would be at this point in your life? Or do you need to start the work of turning your dreams into realities?

> MANY WOMEN DON'T DREAM PAST TODAY BECAUSE THEY HAVE BECOME TOO CAUGHT UP IN THEIR MYRIAD ROLES AND RESPONSIBILITIES.

OVERCOMING OBSTACLES TO TRANSFORMING DREAMS INTO REALITY

For many, the notion of seeing their dreams come to life can be frightening or simply too much to fathom. They've gotten comfortable living a "normal" life with the usual expectations and have adapted to the status quo, feeling hesitant about rocking the boat. In the words of author Brian Tracy:

> The first enemy is the comfort zone. This is the natural tendency of most people to become comfortable and complacent in their current work or lifestyles, and to resist changing in any way. But change is the law of growth, and growth is the law of life. If you don't move out of your comfort zone, you cannot make any progress.

Remember, the more you do what you are doing, the more you will get of what you've got.[23]

Another possible impediment to achieving your dreams may be that you are "playing it small," hesitant to put forth the effort and make the sacrifices you know will be necessary to bring about the fulfillment of your dream. As Aimee Bernstein puts it in her compelling book *Stress Less. Achieve More.*:

> Most people play it small. They just want their problems to be solved and their day-to-day existence to be more comfortable. They want incremental change. Sure, they may say they want the big dream, but they stay on the receiving side of it rather than the creating side. They ask or even plead for what they want rather than affirming that they already have it. Yet, they don't extend their energetic intent or fishing line to that which they desire in order to hook it and live big. In other words, they don't expand their energetic size (not their ego) in order to accommodate the largeness of their dream.[24]

And still other women refuse to reframe their dreams or to reimagine what they want to do with their lives. If a dream seems to have "expired," they fail to renew it or refresh it with a modified version.

As children and adolescents, most of us had dreams of our future selves and the lives we would lead. These childhood dreams got lost in the day-to-day work of adult lives. Some women, in adulthood, take the opportunity to reconnect to the meaning of their dreams, if

---

23. Brian Tracy, *Reinvention: How to Make the Rest of Your Life the Best of Your Life* (New York: American Management Association, 2009), 49.
24. Aimee Bernstein, *Stress Less. Achieve More.: Simple Ways to Turn Pressure into a Positive Force in Your Life* (New York: AMACOM, 2015), 220.

not the exact dreams themselves. They create new, adult dreams to point them in new directions. In shaping our dreams, we must reach inside to find what we want to do, who we want to be, and what we are emotionally committed to, because when dreams include goals that increase personal competence or require new learning, we usually enjoy our efforts or performances. When we pursue activities for their intrinsic interest, simply because we want to, we are likely to become and remain fascinated and absorbed by them. In adults, intrinsic motivation has been shown to contribute to active, productive engagement in work, play, and creative activities. Conversely, when dreams are based on seeking favorable judgments from others, we respond poorly and give up more easily, avoid challenges, experience anxiety, and have lowered self esteem. Concentrating on the external rewards decreases emotional involvement and increases negative feelings. Dreams serve as guides because old dreams may speak to the heart of who we still remain. Even if becoming a rock star is out, tap dancing is in. Dreams do not have to turn into careers; dreams give us back aspects of ourselves that provide joy and satisfaction.[25]

Did you catch that? Dreams "give us back" parts of ourselves that bring us fulfillment. I ask you again: What did you dream of being or doing as a child? How did you feel about that activity or pursuit? What are your dreams, desires, and longings today?

By answering the questions, you can formulate your dreams. Those dreams must be authentic—yours and no one

---

25. Linda N. Edelstein, *The Art of Midlife: Courage and Creative Living for Women* (Westport, CT: Bergin & Garvey, 1999), 196.

else's, personally tailored, so they will motivate you to take action with courage. The future may look uncertain, but it isn't. Through our dreams, we give it definition, and courage allows us to pursue it. Your dreams will go hand in hand with your purpose. Notice that I'm not necessarily urging you to "dream big"; I'm asking that you assess your unique, individual desires for something that motivates and promises to fulfill you.

If you have never approached dreaming in this way—or even if you have, and you've been met only with frustration—I have included the upcoming chapters to help you on your journey. You may not be the biggest dreamer in the world or the most outstanding visionary. Still, you will come to understand that within yourself is a veritable factory of dreams that gave rise to the present and can promise a bright future.

If you're going to dream great dreams and give them a fighting chance to become realities, you must draw on your passion, imagination, and creativity; you must be willing and ready to take risks. Keep your focus on the final destination in your mind because this kind of focus will inspire and empower you. Like the apostle Paul, be able to say, *"Forgetting those things which are behind and reaching forward to those things which are ahead, I press toward the goal for the prize of the upward call of God in Christ Jesus"* (Philippians 3:13–14). A great dream is a fire in your belly that fills you with the desire to make yourself and others better. Are you ready to ignite that fire?

A great dream is a bold vision of the future that both frightens and excites you.

DREAMING IN DETAIL

*T*he fulfillment of our dreams doesn't usually happen overnight. It may take days, months, even years before we see our dreams turned into realities. The longer we have to wait, the greater the chances become that we will grow discouraged and desperate, get stuck, and even give up. As it says in Proverbs 13:12, *"Hope deferred makes the heart sick."* Our time of waiting will test our patience and stretch our faith, but it is well worth enduring because of the second part of that verse, which reads, *"But when the desire comes, it is a tree of life."* We must hold on and hold out for that *"tree of life,"* and there are certain things we can do to help get us through the waiting game.

One of the most effective practices I have found has been a part of my life since I was very young. I didn't read it in a New Age book or hear it from a motivational speaker, although many secular sources validate the concept. It was a revelation I found in the Bible, in the book of Habakkuk:

> And the LORD answered me, and said, Write the vision, and make it plain upon tables, that he may run that readeth it. For the vision is yet for an appointed time, but at the end it shall speak, and not lie: though it tarry, wait for it; because it will surely come, it will not tarry.
>
> (Habakkuk 2:2–3 KJV)

These verses make it clear that although a vision may take some time to manifest, it will ultimately come without a doubt. The author then writes a phrase that Christian believers often quote: "*The just shall live by his faith*" (Habakkuk 2:4 KJV). God was saying, in other words, "You need the vision to know where you are going. And during your time of waiting, your faith will help you."

It is because of Habakkuk 2:2 that, as a young girl, I started recording on my bathroom mirror the things I was waiting for in my life. Later, as a result of further reading and Bible study, I took that habit to a more elaborate level by incorporating images in a practice I now call creating a "dream board." By creating dream boards, I gave myself a place to see, believe, and activate my faith when waiting for a dream to manifest.

WHAT YOU SEE IS WHAT YOU'LL BELIEVE

The Bible gives us this definition of *faith*: "*Now faith is the substance of things hoped for, the evidence of things not seen*" (Hebrews 11:1). When something is unseen in the natural world, we can see it in our imagination and put it on a vision board to bolster our belief.

Even psychology supports what I received years ago as a spiritual principle. In her remarkable book *Building Your Field of Dreams*, Mary Manin Morrissey explains something that struck me the first time I read it. If I were to say to one of my daughters, "Go to your room and get your black shoes," my daughter wouldn't see the word "room" in her mind. She wouldn't say to me, "My room? Mom, what is that?" Any one of my daughters would know what I meant and would go straight to where I'd asked her to go and do what I'd requested. Words create images in our minds that can lead us to the right place.

Have you ever experienced the following situation? Someone asks you for the address of a particular business or residence, and you answer, "I know how to get there, but I don't know how to explain it to you." What happens is that our mind conjures the specific image of the route, and we mentally follow it step-by-step. Our brain can't move in a direction it doesn't know. If you've never gone in that direction, and someone explains how to get there, in your mind, you build the road, and, ideally, when the time comes, you follow the route your mind painted.

The challenge for some people comes when they realize that many of the things they've dreamed of don't have a corresponding image that's concrete. The idea is that when our dreams are not defined but are made up of general phrases like "travel more," "be a better person," and "improve my health," creating a vision board can be a big challenge. For what images would you assign to these dreams? They are conceptual ideas rather than tangible objects. In the pursuit of our dreams, it is up to us to define those concepts and assign them a corresponding image to have a clear picture of what they mean to us.

ASSIGN AN IMAGE TO EACH DREAM

Some of our dreams may come with a detailed image, yet we still don't give them a specific definition. To imagine is nothing more than to think using pictures. Marketing agencies and advertising firms understand this truth. That's why their ad campaigns speak to our minds with vivid images. The power of an advertising campaign is not only what is verbal in the ad. The real value of an advertising campaign is in the image and the emotions it evokes and will capture in the recipient.

It is one thing to desire a house, generally speaking. It is something else to desire a single-story home in a specific urban development with three bedrooms, two bathrooms, and a large patio. The more specific we can be with the images we conceive of for our dreams, the better results we will get as we chase them down. Before we can make our dreams come true, we have to see ourselves experiencing the fulfillment of those dreams. One way to do this is by creating a dream board—by putting an image in front of us and using it as a point of contact where we can see ourselves.

PORTRAY WHAT YOU EXPECT

You can't imagine the difference a dream board made for me during the years my husband and I were fighting in court against two banks in Puerto Rico. I never attended any court hearings, but through my dream board and my prayers, I was present. One day after listening to Otoniel talk at length about the judge, I added several images to my board: a picture of a female judge with a gavel in hand and, next to her, a larger-than-life logo of our church; opposite those, I added tiny logos from the banks. For years, this image was displayed on our bathroom mirror—a personalized picture of Goliath (the banks, represented by no fewer than fourteen law firms) and David (us, with only one lawyer). Despite the advantages of our opponents, my dream board represented our side as being larger and more significant, which bolstered my faith that we would emerge victorious in the end.

The actual course of our court battles didn't always look the way they were portrayed on my dream board. Through the nine years of legal fights and litigation, there were many ups and downs. But in the end, that image we saw every day on my dream board became a reality. With tears in our eyes and unspeakable relief in our hearts, we removed that image from our dream board, giving thanks to the almighty God who had held us during that time. Without that image contributing to our faith, I'm sure those moments of loss would have been even more difficult to bear.

GET SPECIFIC

Every year, I lead the women's Facebook group I've organized through the exercise of building a dream board. Although many women seem to overflow with natural creativity, I am always struck by the number of women in this group who send me messages telling me they have no idea where to start with their dream board. Even if they can list their most pressing desires, when presented with a blank piece of paper, a board, or a wall upon which to portray their dreams, they get stuck, unable to do anything.

Have you ever gone to the supermarket without a list? What happens to you at those times happens to all of us. We forget at least one thing we need while buying multiple items we don't need. Even if we walk right past a pressing item from our list, if we haven't written it down and we don't have our list to consult, we are apt to continue walking without adding the item to our cart. We miss the main thing we went to the store to purchase.

Thanks to God and to advances in technology, I rarely go to the supermarket these days; I do most of my shopping online and have my groceries delivered to my house. But if I'm heading to a store that does not offer online shopping, I usually make sure to take along a list, and I don't get into line for the cashier until I've double-checked that every item on that list has been accounted for without a doubt. This way, I don't waste time walking around aimlessly, exploring every shelf. I go in, get what I need, pay for my purchases, and leave. And that's how we're going to enter our future when we have a dream board completed.

One of the most significant benefits of putting our dreams on a dream board we then display prominently in our home is that it means we have no choice but to think about the future. Many women are stuck living in the past or looking for a way out of their history when the answer is to leave the past behind and start visualizing the future. A dream board is a way of putting your vision on paper.

Today, I urge you to create a dream board of your own. In doing this, you will give yourself a constant reminder of your goals and a concrete image of what you expect. You will also enact a commitment to yourself to never stop believing. Each representation you record will serve you well, giving you material for your meditations and your prayers.

HOW TO CREATE A DREAM BOARD

Before I guide you through creating your dream board, I want to emphasize two important instructions:

+ You must be very clear and specific about your dream: what you want to achieve, why you want to obtain it, how you will achieve it (if you know the "how"), and how you will measure your progress.

+ Your big dream has to be very clear in your mind; you have to be able to see it, taste it, smell it, and articulate it. It must come out of your pores, so to speak.

Now, let's create your dream board step by step.

1. Find a place to exhibit your dream board. A dream board can be something personal that you alone see. In that case, you should display it in a place no one else can access. For example, I keep several smaller boards behind my closet door, an area that not even my husband regularly sees. The key is to make it visible to yourself in a place where you will see it every day.

Suppose your dream board reflects goals you have for your marriage or your entire family. In that case, you will want to place it somewhere more visible, such as on the refrigerator in the kitchen, on the mantel in the family room, in a hallway near the bedrooms, or someplace with similar visibility. For the family, it's not just a reminder; it's a call for commitment from everyone. You have to establish with your family members what they should do with the board every day, whether to pause beside it to pray, to declare Scripture over the dream that's portrayed, or something else. When a family has faith together for something, it's a powerful thing.

In the case of a dream board for your marriage, the master bedroom is ideal for displaying it. Even if your children regularly visit your bedroom, that's okay; they will be able to see that Mom and Dad have a shared vision that represents more than you can imagine. Creating a dream board together with your spouse carries a strong message of unity and bodes a bright future for the family.

Once you have determined whose dreams the board will portray and where you will display the board (or boards, multiple—don't limit yourself to just one board), then...

2. Embody the image of what you dream about. When you take this step, remember that your dream board is your vision of the future. Do not choose pictures representing your present situation, the way you feel today, or the work you are doing now. Portray your dreams for the future, starting with (but not limiting yourself to) these five areas of life:

a. **Wellness:** Remember that wellness covers your physical, emotional, and psychological health, your concept of happiness, and whatever gives you a sense of fulfillment.

b. **Relationships:** Seek to envision how you want your current relationships to look and what new connections you want to make. As you cast a vision for the future of your relationships, be sure to consider your spouse, children, and other family members; your coworkers; your neighbors; your friends; and so forth.

c. **Vocation:** If you are happy in your present occupation, envision the progress you wish to achieve. If your dream is to change your profession and be successful, write it down and look for illustrations of your strongest desires.

d. **Time:** Dreams without deadlines are just goals that you're unlikely to achieve. Every dream on your board should be assigned a corresponding completion date.

e. **Finances:** Don't be limited by what others call the "realities of life" when you establish your financial dreams.

Clarify your aspirations in terms of salary, earnings, or income, even if you don't know where you're going to get it. Go for your biggest dreams.

3. Take the time to write down everything you want. Write a detailed description of what the ultimate fulfillment of your goal looks like to you. What kind of person will you be at the end of your dream? Visualize this future reality and observe it intently in your mind's eye. Look carefully at all the things you would be doing at that moment, and let this image guide your path.

If your dream board is related to family, it will be a helpful experience—and, I hope, an enjoyable one—for everyone to contribute their unique visions and dreams. I recommend designating a parent moderator because these family conversations can become chaotic if there is no leadership, especially in larger families. Keep the goal in mind: painting a picture of the future to help the whole family believe.

As you make a list of specific components of your dream, certain key phrases and images will emerge that you can then capture on the board, making them easier to conceive of and achieve. For example, you might write down "$10 million in revenue by [such date]." You can be like comedian Jim Carrey, who, in 1985, wrote himself a check dated Thanksgiving 1995 for the amount of $10 million for "acting services rendered," as he recorded on the memo line. This he did while dreaming of entertaining the world with his comedic skills. Just before the date he had written on the check, Carrey signed a contract for his role in the movie *Dumb and Dumber*, for which he was paid exactly $10 million.[26]

---

26. Pawan Kumar, "What I learned from Jim Carrey—Who Wrote Himself a $10 Million Check," *ART + Marketing.com*, October 2, 2017, https:// artplusmarketing.com/what-i-learned-from-jim-carrey-fc6fbb2c0620.

Your dream board may be filled with words and sentences alone, but in my experience, a dream board is much more exciting, eye-catching, and effective when it also includes images. I cannot emphasize enough that you make your visual representation with real images—whether photos taken by you or pictures printed from the Internet or cut from a magazine—that represent what you want. If you dream of a vacation, collect photos of the place you want to visit. If you dream of getting married, display a couple in wedding attire or a wedding party. If you envision starting a business, find photos that capture the way you see your future office or the essence of the product or service you plan to sell. The reality is that, in terms of capturing images, your creativity is your only limit. In the past, I used pictures that I cut out of magazines or photos taken by myself. Every time I came across something I could use, I would cut it out and paste it on my board. Today, the Internet and home printers make this task much more feasible.

4. Assemble your dream board as a collage of the essential phrases and images you have identified and collected. Many people focus on making their boards beautiful, and there is nothing wrong with that. But, more than making it beautiful, you should...

5. Seek to make your dream board meaningful. The idea is that when you look at your dream board, your emotions will be touched, your motivation will be moved, and the sight will ignite a flame inside you that will keep you fighting and believing for the eventual fulfillment of those dreams.

Don't put so much material on the board that it becomes difficult to see the individual components and recall what they represent. Once again, you have to see this board as your blueprint for the future. How do you build a house? It requires a drawing, an outline, a plan. As you build that house, perhaps there's nothing there, but then you lay the foundation. You lay the house's skeleton until it's formed, and you don't see it in the natural world; many people think it didn't exist. Of course, it did! That plan and that drawing show that it did exist in the mind of an engineer or architect who drew it. Your dream board is that drawing. It shows you the final result of what you expect to happen.

6. When you're done, analyze your dream board. Ask yourself: "Does my dream board contain everything I'm believing for?" "Is it clear enough so that, with one look, I get the right picture?" "Is it strategically located to be part of my daily life?" "Is the material I've used durable enough to withstand the time I'll need to wait?" You want the work you've done to pay off, and there's no way of knowing how long you'll keep any particular words or images on your board before those dreams are fulfilled.

7. Update your dream board as needed. When you see any aspect of your dreams come to fruition, be sure to do something special to mark the occasion. If you notice that something is missing, or if you find that one of your images is no longer having the effect it should, make the necessary changes. Your vision board needs to evoke in you such feelings as motivation and joy. It needs to put you "in the mood" for action.

Some people prepare a new dream board every year. Making an annual dream board allows you to analyze your progress year by year, but you can create as many boards as you want to, as often as you see fit. The idea of renewing or analyzing your dream board year by year is excellent. However, make sure you are not changing your dreams every year. Don't let the frustration you may feel when you see another year go by without your achieving something specific change your commitment to that dream.

8. Pay attention to your dream board. No matter how effective an advertising campaign may be, a big company will invest millions of dollars to make it even more productive, emotional, and penetrating. Please don't make a dream board only to set it aside without giving it the attention, care, and follow-up that it requires. Paying attention to your dream board can make such a difference in your dreams. I have read hundreds of biographies and heard countless success stories of people who had in common the practice of creating and referring to a vision board.

For your dream board to inhabit the deepest parts of your mind and heart, pay attention to it every chance you get. The most effective practice I have found, and one that enhances my spiritual life, too, is to pray about my dream board. During your prayer time, refer to your board and declare God's Word over each area it represents. I can't think of a better place to pray in your house than in front of your dream board.

The reality is that, time and again, the Lord uses images, through His Word, to project a future vision and keep His people focused. He gave Abraham the sand by day and the stars by night to visualize the innumerable descendants he would eventually have. (See Genesis 22:17; 26:4.) What God never does is put an image of the past before you.

In addition to creating a dream board, develop a mind-vision map for your dream. Your big idea should make you feel excited and scared at the same time. Close your eyes, move purposefully into the future, and imagine that you have achieved your dream. How will you feel when that happens?

MAKE A DREAM BOARD THAT SPEAKS TO YOU

I like to make my dream boards big, flashy, and colorful because that's my personality. Your visual representation should speak to you. It should be striking to you according to your taste and personality. If you don't like glitter, you don't have to put glitter on your dream board just because others do. Paint, cut out, and paste that which results in a message that allows you to see your destiny expressed clearly and powerfully.

If you would prefer to create a digital dream board, you may choose to create a slide on your computer or tablet that displays pictures of your dream. You could also create a series of photos to be displayed in a digital picture frame.

IF YOU KEEP ON RELIVING THE PAST, YOU CAN'T ENVISION THE GLORIOUS FUTURE THAT GOD HAS FOR YOU.

One significant effect of your dream board will be to draw your gaze and attract your attention away from your past so that you focus on the future. If you keep on reliving the past, you can't envision the glorious future that God has for you. Just as you cannot move in one direction without definition, you cannot move in two directions simultaneously. Instead of analyzing your past, reason your way into your future. There is nothing to look at in your past; focus on your future. For that, your vision board is your secret weapon. Create one now, and don't look back anymore!

Every broken dream

is an opportunity

for growth.

Chapter 9

DON'T GIVE UP ON YOUR DREAM

Love Like You've Never Been Hurt is the title of a recent book by one of my favorite preachers, Jentezen Franklin. However, most people don't know the compelling story of the sentiment behind this memorable title. The statement was first uttered by Leroy Robert "Satchel" Paige, a professional baseball player who certainly endured his share of hurts, including racism, abuse, poverty, and segregation. Due to the strictures of racial discrimination, he didn't reach the big leagues until he was forty-one years of age. He pitched until age fifty-nine, setting a record that is unlikely to be broken by any other baseball player. In spite of the discriminatory views of society at large and even some of his teammates, he left a legacy that proves it is possible to overcome even the severest offenses in the most challenging circumstances. Satchel Paige taught us that you should always show a humble and generous heart.[27]

Following in the steps of Satchel Paige is far easier said than done, however. The truth is, the deepest wounds we suffer are inflicted by those closest to us—parents, siblings, spouses, children, and intimate friends. How difficult it is to heal a wounded soul! A broken bone or another type of injury to the flesh usually has a corresponding medical remedy that will cure the affliction if you follow your doctor's orders and allow enough time for healing. Even for medical issues with no cure, there are usually ways of experiencing relief from pain and discomfort. But the wounds of the soul play to a different tune.

DON'T DWELL ON PAST PAINS

In my years of ministry, I have lost count of the number of people I have counseled who had been offended and gravely wounded by the words and actions of someone close to them. Each of us probably carries the memory of painful experiences and relational rifts that we can't seem to shake, no matter what we try. How I wish we could enjoy selective amnesia, remembering only the happy moments in life and forgetting all misfortune. Sadly, even more than negative memories, I have seen people carry around with them inner hells, continually filled with anger, resentment, and hatred against the people who hurt their feelings or disappointed them in a big way.

As long as we direct our attention to these painful experiences—mentally dwelling on them, rehashing them in our conversations—we keep the wounds fresh and raw rather than allowing them to transform into scars. Maybe you know someone who regularly talks about a painful experience from their

---

27. Andrew Webb, "Love like you've never been hurt," The Spark, June 4, 2018, https://www.thespark.org.uk/love-like-youve-never-been-hurt/.

past. Perhaps you make a habit of doing this. We've all done it at some point. Some ministry friends of mine were hurt by another couple's departure from their ministry. For years after this departure, the wounded couple talked only about how ungrateful the other couple had been, the hurtful things they had said, or the offensive comment or photo posted on Facebook. This couple seemed incapable of having a discussion about anything else. Even if they talked about another matter, the conversation always drifted back to this dramatic split. This repetitive speech pattern befalls many women who insist on talking about their ex-husband, their ex-worker, and, unfortunately, even their ex-family. They dredge up and verbally rehash the same negative experience over and over again. And my message to such people is always the same: Your wounds are not going to heal if you keep on opening them with your words and thoughts.

YOUR EMOTIONAL WOUNDS ARE NOT GOING TO HEAL IF YOU KEEP ON OPENING THEM WITH YOUR WORDS AND THOUGHTS.

The wounds of humiliation, disappointment, rejection, betrayal, and loss are inevitable in a world governed by the sinful nature of humankind. Yet we often magnify the hurts we experience by refusing to forgive, let go, and move on. We mistakenly feel that we will somehow punish those who harmed us by holding on to bitterness and anger. Or we may say, "I'll forgive others only when they acknowledge their wrongdoing and apologize for it." These stances only trap us in the pain of our wounds, preventing us from experiencing the power of pardoning our offenders as God has pardoned us. That is why the Bible's teachings on the importance of extending forgiveness are so comprehensive.

In one of His teachings on forgiveness, Jesus's disciples asked Him how many times they needed to forgive an offender. He answered, *"I do not say to you, up to seven times, but up to seventy times seven"* (Matthew 18:22). Never pretending to be an expert in biblical numerology, I have to say that there are many theological proposals of what that means. Some say it must have been seventy-seven. Others claim that it would be seventy times seven—that is, four hundred and ninety. Still other theologians insist that it corresponds to the infinite number formed by putting seven, seventy times in a row. That is a number that would take about twenty-three commas to separate. Anyway, without taking away or agreeing with any of them, I have to say that the number Jesus gave is usually far higher than the number of times the average person wants to forgive those who have wounded their soul.

Along our life's journey, we are bound to be offended by others. And we are wrong if we think we can solve anything by forcing an apology or demanding an explanation. The reality is that we can be free of the suffering we experience at the hands of others who don't value us. When we decide to forgive, regardless of any apology we may have heard or any appearance of a penitent heart, we restore our dignity by extending forgiveness. Extend pardon and put an end to your agony by leaving the matter in the past. When you value yourself and your dreams because you know how valuable you are to the One who gave them to you, you rise above needing the acceptance and affirmation of other people.

REFUSE TO CALL IT QUITS

All of us have failed and fallen short at some point, but that doesn't have to signify the death of our dreams. Failure is a temporary frustration of our goals, accompanied by strong feelings; but it need not be a permanent state. Mistakes, stumbles, and backward steps may be an unavoidable part of our journey, but they should never become the end of the road.

If you allow a personal failure to stop you in your tracks, you won't fulfill your purpose or adapt to your shortcomings in a way that will enable you to reach your dreams despite them. Your life can and should become precisely the life God has and wants for you. No matter what failures you may experience, you can continue to pursue God's will for every season of your life—a will that makes room for mistakes and can use all things for our ultimate good. (See Romans 8:28.) The apostle Paul put it this way: *"Not as though I had already attained, either were already perfect: but I follow after, if that I may apprehend that for which also I am apprehended of Christ Jesus"* (Philippians 3:12 KJV).

By practicing perseverance and cultivating a can-do attitude, you can continue to pursue your dreams despite any failures! The apostle Paul traveled a long way by the hand of God and encountered many setbacks, including prison sentences and shipwrecks. Yet he persevered and did not give up because he knew God wasn't finished with him. Woman, the same can be true for you. A delay is not the end of your job. Rise from your failures and develop the commitment to keep going until you accomplish and reach all that you have set out to do. Emulate the apostle Paul, forgetting that which has passed and focusing only on what is ahead. (See Philippians 3:13.)

Permit yourself to acknowledge failure, but never allow yourself to refuse to try again. Those who give up on their dreams are doomed to bury them, live a life of frustration, and look to the past with probing questions that have no answers, like, "Why did such and such have to happen?" and "Why did things have to be this way?" Queries such as those are futile and fruitless, only bringing frustration and reducing our motivation to try again. The only question worth asking is, What can I do differently to produce a better outcome in the future? When you stumble and fall, don't put up a wall in front of you. Let it be a fence that you strive to jump over. The path to your destiny and dreams will always have obstacles you must overcome. With the right attitude and a strong commitment, you have what it takes!

OVERCOMING OBSTACLES WITH THE PROPER PERSPECTIVE

Every broken dream is an opportunity for growth. Think about a time when you failed at something. What did you discover about yourself through that experience? Our falls and failures help us identify our capabilities and refine our strengths in ways that otherwise would have been inaccessible. There is always something to learn from a negative experience. Because of that, even our failures can be valuable. Even in the worst of times, you can learn something new about yourself and become better equipped to tackle similar situations in the future. You can use your newfound wisdom to strengthen your abilities and be prepared the next time you set out in pursuit of a dream.

Never assume that your journey has ended just because you've hit a stumbling block. Every challenge you meet and every obstacle you come across can bring you closer to your dream if you'll only adopt the proper perspective and refuse to quit. Even when something seems impossible, women from every walk of life have proved repeatedly that the way to succeed is by holding fast to your dreams and not giving up. All around us are women who stand up for themselves and their beliefs while pursuing their dreams. These women refuse to allow obstacles and failures to bring them down. Every time they fell, they got back up and resumed the pursuit of their dreams.

EVERY CHALLENGE YOU MEET AND EVERY OBSTACLE YOU COME ACROSS CAN BRING YOU CLOSER TO YOUR DREAM IF YOU'LL ONLY ADOPT THE PROPER PERSPECTIVE AND REFUSE TO QUIT.

Today, you become one of those women. If you've convinced yourself that you will never achieve what you desire, the time has come to convince yourself otherwise. If you've found yourself laughing at the notion of your dream coming true, I challenge you to sober up and adopt an attitude of hopeful expectation. It's just that the time appointed by God has not come. His promises are true, and He always arrives just in time.[28] Instead of classifying yourself as either a success or a failure, identify yourself as a woman who won't give up on her dreams and won't stop pursuing her destiny. You may know plenty of other people who were stopped in their tracks by a series of setbacks, but you're not going to be one of them. Wake up each day with the courage that comes from knowing that within you is the strength to keep going and continue trying until you reach all your dreams. With God, there is no countdown, and it is never

---

28. Joyce Meyer, *You Can Begin Again: No Matter What, It's Never Too Late* (New York: FaithWords, 2015), 41–42.

too late.[29] Even if you think your journey has ended, remember that every obstacle you encounter can bring you closer to achieving your dream.

WITHSTAND COMMON DREAM KILLERS

Are you living a life that feels incomplete because of something you desperately want that hasn't happened yet? You longed for a happy marriage, but your husband left you. You've dreamed your whole life of having a baby, but you haven't conceived. You started a business that failed. You thought you'd be together forever, but the person you loved passed away. You've tried and tried to heal a relationship, but it's still broken. You gave years of your life to a career aspiration that hasn't worked out the way you envisioned. The important thing is not to fall prey to what I call "dream killers"—erroneous assumptions that can keep us from trying again after a setback.

FALLACIES ABOUT AGE

Amid situations like these, many women consider their age or calculate how long things seem to be taking and say, "It's too late." Time awareness is very different between men and women for many reasons. Still, I think the primary reason is the biological clock and the various implications for both sexes. Early on in youth, women begin to experience the pressure to have children sooner rather than later. That pressure marks our life's calendar and causes us to look at time differently. Many women shape their life's plan around childbearing, mapping out what they will do before having children, while raising their children, and after their children have left the nest. In many families, the mother shoulders the primary responsibilities of parenting, postponing many dreams for the "after children"

---

29. Meyer, *You Can Begin Again*, 35.

part of their lives—only to feel as if it's too late once they reach that point.

We need to silence the telltale ticking of the so-called biological clock. I had my first daughter at twenty-two and my second daughter at twenty-four, and then God blessed me with two more daughters at the ages of thirty-five and thirty-seven. In the United States, any pregnancy for a woman over thirty-five years of age is considered high risk. In my case, however, my overall health was the same across all four pregnancies, regardless of my age. I felt more energetic and robust during my pregnancies in my mid- to late thirties than I did when pregnant as a twenty-something-year-old.

In Spain, 30 percent of women have their first child after age thirty-five. This statistic makes me think that the pressure that American women feel to have children before the age of thirty is due to manipulating thoughts that do not have women's best interests at heart.

A woman shouldn't have children until she has married a reliable man with whom she can partner in raising their off-spring. She also needs to feel comfortable about the idea of being a mother. I did not say she needs to be "ready" because every parent can attest that no one is ever 100 percent ready to be a mother or a father. So, by feeling comfortable with the idea and having the right attitude and desire to learn all the way, I think you have a big part of the battle won. A woman should have children in her own time. Please ignore the pressure that your family may put on you or society's opinion on when it's appropriate to have children. Don't let anyone put pressure on you to become a mother in the first place!

The same goes for studies and advances in professional life. For some reason, we think that we can only study in our youth, another great fallacy that puts pressure on women more than on men. A friend of mine told me that she wanted to study, but the thought of being in a classroom with young people who might be the same age as her own children—or even younger than her children—frightened her. She feared that her more youthful peers would look down on her and devalue her presence and contributions. I believe she developed this fear because her own children did look down on her; it was a feeling she knew all too well and did not want to experience elsewhere.

WE NEED TO SILENCE THE TICKING OF THE SO-CALLED BIOLOGICAL CLOCK.

Today, thanks to technology and the changes we have seen in educational options, there are adult-oriented programs that fit the needs of modern women very well—even those who have children to raise. Thirty years ago, studying, preparing for a professional career, and working outside the home would have been a challenging, almost impossible, scenario for a mother. But not so today.

Even so, many women bury their dreams because of age, time, the struggle to find a balance between the demands of motherhood and the challenges of a professional career, or something else. Men don't feel the same pressure about their biological clock; they don't struggle with fertility the older they get in the way women do. Besides those men who have a conscience about not wanting to raise children after a certain age, the rest aren't counting how many years they have left to be able to father children. On top of that, they don't have to regularly interrupt their professional life for marriage, children, or parenting. We women are the ones who mostly find ourselves making those sacrifices or being criticized or judged by the people closest to us for not doing so.

The truth is that we live in a world governed by time. It's okay to set specific goals and be responsible stewards of the time God gives us. However, when we are overly conscious of time constraints, we tend to live in a hurry, full of stress and trying to fulfill our plans in what we've been told is the "reasonable" time frame for doing things. We start living with unnecessary burdens that were never God's intent because He desires only good for us. I think this is one reason why many people miss out on their dreams—they don't strive to reach them because they feel it's too late. They bury their dreams prematurely, falling prey to the false notion of time constraints dictated by society.

JOKES THAT SCAR US

In his book *The Joke and Its Relation to the Unconscious*, Sigmund Freud probes the essence of, and the motives behind, those everyday jokes that most of us laugh off. However, for the famous psychoanalyst, a joke is far more than just an intelligent or sympathetic way of discharging emotional tension. Freud explains that people tend to present what they perceive to be the realities of life through jokes. Instead of openly affirming what one thinks, jokes reduce unconsciously held concepts using laughter and tension. According to Sigmund Freud, every joke covers up a truth.

Consider, for example, the infamous mother-in-law joke. Most of these jokes present mothers-in-law as inconsiderate, intrusive, and problematic women. Is that the reality of all mothers-in-law? Of course not. But those stories and jokes had to come from somewhere. Somehow, the attitudes of many mothers-in-law gave way to the concepts that we have come to associate with them because of mother-in-law jokes.

Have you ever stopped to analyze the themes behind any of the jokes that allude to women? In many jokes, women are portrayed as bossy, meddlesome, and/or perfectionistic, either clinging to or suffocating their husbands and children. Is that the absolute reality of all women? No. On the contrary, as I argue in my book *Midwife of Dreams*, many women are instrumental in pushing their loved ones to reach their full potential. Behind countless success stories are the women who propelled and encouraged those successful individuals in crucial ways. Women have proven themselves indispensable instruments to compel, motivate, and lead others to produce excellent results in all areas.

Still other jokes present women as frustrated individuals. But this portrayal is no laughing matter. The Global Dreams Index Survey questioned 5,400 women in fourteen countries across six continents and reported that more than 50 percent of women had given up on their dreams as children and felt dissatisfied with their lives.[30] It may shock and even annoy us that many jokes present women as frustrated. The reality is that while a woman can be an excellent cheerleader for everyone else's dreams, data shows that she does not do the same for herself.

For most women, dreams are silly, unrealistic, not things "grown-ups" have time to entertain. Whether it's a demanding career or a hectic family life, we all come to accept that a head in the clouds gets in the way of the

---

30. Shihab S. Joi, "1 in 2 Women Have Given Up On Their True Dream," *Huffpost*, June 23, 2016, https://www.huffingtonpost.co.uk/entry/what-it-takes-to-achieve-a-childhood-dream_uk_5767f36ee4b01fb65863d502.

job at hand. As a result, many of us let go of our dreams altogether.[31]

Jokes about women reveal the stereotypes and pervasive impressions that many women fall prey to and allow to limit their dreams without ever questioning them or seeking to defy them.

OTHER PEOPLE'S OPINIONS

A report printed in *Forbes* magazine entitled "Why Most Women Give Up on Their Dreams" lists the following three primary reasons women fail to fulfill their dreams: lack of support, financial limitations, and lack of self-confidence.[32] A significant factor in most people's level of self-confidence is their perception of the opinions of others. A woman who pursues her dreams must be able to believe in herself, regardless of what she thinks other people think about what she's doing.

Still, in many areas of our lives, we are limited by the opinions of others. Many women are terrified of criticism and avoid, at all costs, clashing with others' lifestyles and beliefs. Everybody likes to be liked.

When we decide to do something radically different from what we have been doing, we can expect the people closest to us to have an opinion. When that opinion is different from yours, instead of giving more weight to what those other people think, you should say to yourself, "That's their opinion, but I think differently." Dare to believe in yourself, even when others doubt you. The healthiest self-confidence does not hinge on the

---

31. Joi, "1 in 2 Women Have Given Up On Their True Dream."
32. Soulaima Gourani, "Why Most Women Give Up On Their Dreams," *Forbes*, July 30, 2019, https://www.forbes.com/sites/soulaimagourani/2019/07/29/why-most-women-give-up-on-their-dreams/#3ad9cb402082.

opinions of others, though I acknowledge how difficult it is not to allow those opinions to overshadow our aspirations.

STAGES OF THE DEATH OF A DREAM

Like any death, the death of a dream signals multiple stages of grief. If you've ever seen an idea of yours expire before conception, these stages may seem familiar. I've adopted this progression from Joyce Meyer, who explains it beautifully in her book *You Can Begin Again.*

The first stage is *denial.* You may lie to yourself, saying that you never really wanted that dream in the first place.

The second stage is *anger.* This feeling comes on when you begin to think, "It's not fair that others have succeeded while I've had to give up on my plans, desires, and dreams."

The third stage is *bargaining or negotiating.* Here, you may pray, "God, if You would only make _____ happen, I'll stop doing _____." In doing this, you forget that God is not a genie in a bottle guaranteed to grant your wishes. You also deny the effort that is needed on your part to bring your dream to fruition.

The next stage is *depression.* In this stage, we think, "I'm a failure. My dream is dead. My life is terrible. What a waste!"

Finally comes *acceptance.* At this point, you can only say, "Oh, well. It's never going to happen. It's too late."

If you think that any of your hopes, dreams, plans, and ambitions will operate precisely according to your schedule, you will always be disappointed. And even if you could order the fulfillment of your dreams on demand, there would always be an inner countdown and an inescapable fear of being too late. Worse yet, even if you feel confident enough to bet on yourself, there will always be someone reminding you of the "ticking time clock" or to point out all the people who had accomplished so much more by the time they were your age.

When submitted to God by a heart that trusts in God's timing, those same hopes, dreams, plans, and ambitions are guaranteed to come back to life. In the same way that Ezekiel prophesied to the valley of dry bones and raised an army to life again (see Ezekiel 37:1–14), you can revive your dreams by exposing them to the breath of God. The soldiers were without breath at first, saying, *"Our bones are dry, our hope is lost, and we ourselves are cut off"* (Ezekiel 37:11). But God said to them, *"Behold, O My people, I will open your graves and cause you to come up from your graves…I will put My Spirit in you, and you shall live, and I will place you in your own land"* (Ezekiel 37:12, 14). God can revive our dead dreams like no one else. But keep in mind the reason He does so; it's the same reason He breathed life into the dry bones: *"…[so that] you shall know that I, the* LORD, *have spoken it and performed it"* (Ezekiel 37:14). God revives our dreams for our fulfillment and His glory.

There's a "word" you're going to have to speak over your dreams. Why consent to burying your thoughts and letting them go for petty reasons? Many things in our lives compete for our time. But I tell you today that you must not bury your dreams, thinking that their time has expired. Your dreams do not expire like the milk in your fridge or the bread on your countertop. Your goals are much more, and they go far beyond your age and the stage of life you are in right now.

YOUR "JUST TOO LATE" IS GOD'S "JUST IN TIME"

Your "too late to have a family" or "too late to prepare professionally" is God's "just in time" for you to do those things.

Time, age, or the season of our life are not enough reasons to bury our dreams. The God I serve loves to do things that we may assume are impossible or out of time.

God's thoughts are not your thoughts, and His ways are not your ways. (See Isaiah 55:8.) In other words, God's timing is different from your chronological boundaries, and you must pay attention to Him above all else. With Him, there is no such thing as "too late." With God, the worst or best situation becomes a "just in time." That is, God always appears at the right time.[33]

Today, you may have to make a few edits to get your dreams out of the grave. Don't be afraid to adjust your goals so that they can become feasible in your present circumstances. A goal can change, adapt, and evolve. Your "just in time" can come with an edited dream. Take your vision out of the grave, analyze it, adjust it as needed, and run for it. The time to fulfill it is now.

Don't be like the lazy servant in the parable of the talents who buried his talent rather than multiply it for his master's good. (See Matthew 25:14–30.) Be like the other two servants, who were commended for their faithfulness in putting their talents to work and receiving a good return on them. Don't bury your dream but exhume it and pursue it, regardless of what you may have been told about it being "too late" or your being "too old." Devote your time and talents to the pursuit of your dreams so that you can be found a good and faithful woman in the eyes of your master, our Lord. He will give you your reward.

---

33. See Joyce Meyer, *You Can Begin Again*, 36–37.

A worthwhile dream

demands high levels of energy.

Be sure to eat well, exercise,

and get adequate sleep.

EQUIPPED FOR THE COSTS
OF COMMITMENT

$\mathcal{J}$'ll never forget the first time my daughter Jenibelle placed an order online. She wanted a toy that was not available in Puerto Rico, and we had found it on a website. We placed the order, and I was feeling proud of myself for being a resourceful mom. Later that afternoon, Jenibelle asked me with a tone of annoyance, "Mom, where is my toy?" She was expecting her toy to arrive that very day. I explained to her that she had to wait for someone to receive the order, pack her toy, put it on a truck, load it on a plane, and unload it onto another truck to deliver it to our house. The entire process would take several days. All my excitement over being the "international toy-finding mom" was gone in an instant.

Sometimes it seems like the world spins faster for us than it did for our ancestors. Maybe Jenibelle's expectation was unrealistic, but when you think about it, many things that I had to wait for as a child are now available in a moment for my daughters. When I was Jenibelle's age, I had to wait for the DJ on the radio to play my favorite songs; and then, if I was feeling resourceful, I might record those songs on a blank cassette tape. Today, my daughters can download their favorite songs within seconds. The reality is that they were born into a world where we have access to an ocean of instant products, services, and activities at our fingertips. We are blessed with instant gratification in many areas of our lives. But along with that so-called blessing, we also have the disadvantage of forgetting that not everything in life can be instantaneous.

THE PRICE OF PATIENT PERSEVERANCE

Many of us have been seduced by the fruits of instant gratification. Who doesn't want to eat as much as one wants and slim down and get abs with just a daily pill or cup of tea, or by spending only three minutes, three times a week, working out with a "magic machine"? Our lust for instant gratification is the reason we tend to fall for the promises of those infamous TV infomercials that air when we ought to be asleep. It often ceases to be about the need we want to fill but the speed with which we can fulfill it.

We should always keep in mind the wisdom of Ecclesiastes 3:1: *"To everything there is a season, a time for every purpose under heaven."* If we are going to achieve our dreams, we need to understand that everything has its own time and hour. Not every dream can be met in an instant. Nor would we want it to, most likely! Worthwhile dreams usually demand time and energy. Sure, we may hear stories of talented people who were discovered at the right time and rose to stardom overnight; we may read of those who, by a divine encounter, had a problem solved or an obstacle overcome instantaneously. But most good things in life don't come without at least some effort on our part—plus some (or a lot of) waiting.

For many women, sacrificing in the present for the sake of a better future means waiting longer than they feel comfortable doing. So they settle for "mediocre" and "sufficient," depriving themselves of God's best. When we have only our immediate situation in mind—when we lose sight of our long-term goals—we may quickly lose our resolve to make the necessary sacrifices and put forth the adequate effort. For example, many women are longing for a happy marriage to a good man so much so that they will get together with the first man to come along because they fear missing out and spending years alone. Still other women could advance in their careers and receive more competitive salaries if they would only complete their studies or earn a secondary degree, yet they continue to do more work for mediocre pay because they aren't willing to give up their nights or weekends to study. And then, there are women at risk of diabetes, obesity, heart disease, and related issues who refuse to pay the price of better nutrition and regular exercise to help their bodies combat avoidable problems. For them, it is easier to live with the frustration and anxiety of not achieving their dreams than to strive for their goals and give it their all.

THE PRICE OF ERADICATING EXHAUSTION

All of us have probably experienced the failure to achieve a dream due to our exhaustion. Many women exist in a state of perpetual exhaustion—physical, mental, and/or emotional. When our exhaustion outweighs our motivation, we seek that which brings us immediate pleasure, forgetting that hanging in there and working hard in spite of our fatigue will get us more significant rewards in the long run. We need to practice perseverance and endurance if we are going to achieve our dreams. When you have a big dream, you can't expect to resolve it with a mentality that says, "I want it, and I want it now." We all have to work to achieve our dreams, and we are so exhausted with so many issues that the thought of working hard at "something else" discourages us.

> **WHEN YOU HAVE A BIG DREAM, YOU CAN'T EXPECT TO RESOLVE IT WITH A MENTALITY THAT SAYS, "I WANT IT, AND I WANT IT NOW."**

To persevere in the pursuit of your dreams, you have to eradicate exhaustion as much as possible. And a key to eliminating fatigue is to discover that which motivates you at a heart level. Successful people seem to have this in common: a high energy level that stems from their intrinsic motivation and authentic enthusiasm over that which they are striving for in their life. Those who do not have that energy lack motivation, and their lives prove as much, having little to show for their efforts.

Other people often remark on the high energy level I project. Indeed, I have always been generally positive, upbeat, and cheerful—three attributes I consider key to my hardworking nature. I also gravitate toward other people who have the same energy and zeal for worthwhile work. Accordingly, I limit the time I spend with listless, apathetic, pessimistic individuals. If there is something I want, I don't care how hard I have to work for it. If a listless person next to me is in the middle of trying to do something, God bless! They found someone who's going to push them until they get it. That's the energy I project.

Your energy level is a determining factor in every area of your life. That's why it's important to take care of your body and fuel it properly with food and rest. Don't be one of those women who wakes up tired, goes to work tired, and comes home twice as tired at the end of the day. Fatigue may cause you to lie to yourself and think you lack motivation. Countless women have complained to me of their failures, saying, "I just don't have anyone to motivate me." You don't need a bunch of cheerleaders surrounding you. You just need a strong desire and the energy to go after it.

Let me put in a word of caution regarding products promising an energy boost. Many of the pills, drinks and "superfoods" that claim to recharge your batteries are nothing more than superficial remedies with short-term results for your energy—and long-term consequences for your health.

You must implement three elements to have adequate energy for achieving your dreams: quality rest, proper nutrition, and regular physical activity. For many women, a lack of proper rest, a poor diet, and a sedentary lifestyle are the culprits behind their energy shortage. The solution lies in establishing the right habits and being faithful to practice them. The benefits of quality rest, proper nutrition, and regular physical activity are too many to list here. Still, I will share how my life improved when I worked on the area of sleep, in particular.

ADEQUATE REST

My husband, Otoniel, has always been a good sleeper. When we first married, I was amazed at how he could put his head on the pillow and fall asleep instantly. I was the opposite, tending to have a hard time sleeping. I always got up very early, usually at four in the morning, and went to bed late because my day was filled with many responsibilities. Otoniel would tell me, again and again, "Omayra, you have to sleep more." My answer was always the same: "Sleeping is for lazy people." How wrong I was!

Still, it took me a while to teach myself how to sleep in a way that kept my body balanced and energized. I honestly didn't feel as if I lacked energy, probably because of the adrenaline that accompanied the reward of my hard work. But I did begin to puzzle over how my husband slept soundly and woke up rested. So, I started reading about ways to improve one's sleep. And it wasn't long before a good night's sleep became a dream of mine. It may sound outrageous, but sleeping well became my heart's desire.

To achieve this dream, I had to make many changes to my daily routine. These included avoiding screens (TV, phone) before bed, making my bedroom into a sanctuary of rest, heading to bed earlier at night, and even napping during the day.

It was very motivating to read Arianna Huffington's account of how learning to sleep had changed her life.[34] When we are naturally productive people, we may think that sleep is a waste of time or that we don't need it. Today, I have become like Arianna Huffington, a zealous advocate of sleep. I finally recognize that sleep is just as important as food and drink, as Kelly Bulkeley points out in her work on dreams:

> You *need* to sleep. Sleeping is just as essential to your healthy existence as food or water. When you become tired it feels good to sleep, just as it feels good to eat when you're hungry and drink when you're thirsty. Conversely, it feels painful when you don't get enough

---

34. See Arianna Huffington, *The Sleep Revolution: Transforming Your Life, One Night at a Time* (New York: Harmony Books, 2016).

sleep. Just as you can die from lack of food or water, you would not last long if you were completely prevented from sleeping. When laboratory animals are deprived of all sleep they perish in a matter of days.[35]

NUTRITIOUS FOOD

Just as we need to make sure we're getting ample *quality* sleep, we must pay attention to our diets and ensure we're giving ourselves proper nutrition. Some time ago, I adopted a ketogenic diet (keto, for short) to help ease a stomach issue. Of all the changes that I've noticed in my body due to this particular regime—one that eliminates refined flour and sugar—I have to say that increased energy has been the most dramatic. I don't like to recommend specific diets, and I'm not a doctor trying to make any particular dietary recommendations for you. I can only say that, for me, the keto diet has worked excellently. And I can tell you that if you don't eat a balanced diet of nutritious foods, you won't have the energy you need to pursue your dreams.

As children, most of us were told, "Eat well so you'll grow"; "Finish your plate." But once the metabolism of their growing-up years has slowed, many people start counting calories, potentially depriving themselves of the fuel they need if they've chosen to follow low-calorie diets. The foods we select should be high in both nutritional value and energy value. Suppose a diet is too restrictive in terms of calories or a particular nutrient. In that case, you may experience decreases in energy that feel terrible and may prompt you to break with the diet—and possibly boomerang, overdoing it on all the wrong foods.

35. Kelly Bulkeley, *Dreaming in the World's Religions: A Comparative History* (New York: New York University Press, 2008), 1.

You may be thinking, "Pastor, why are you talking about food when you're supposed to be talking about dreams?" The reason is that the food we eat is a vital part of our being and contributes significantly to the energy we can draw on as we strive to reach our dreams.

REGULAR EXERCISE

To anyone who tells me, "I don't have the energy to exercise," I say, "You don't have energy because you don't exercise." Exercising supplies oxygen to the body and boosts the cardiovascular system. If your heart and lungs are fit, your body will have enough energy. It's as simple as that. Exercise also releases endorphins—natural mood boosters—and relieves stress, which can help us to sleep better.

I have been working out routinely since age twelve. I have never exercised to "look fit"; instead, my passion for exercise has always been because of how I feel when I'm physically active. I've participated in many different sports and taken various exercise classes. Most recently, I've taken up running, and I'm preparing for my very first marathon.

As with anything else, it takes time to train one's body and improve in such areas as flexibility, strength, and endurance. Nobody becomes a bodybuilder or a marathon athlete overnight. But we all can start somewhere, doing something. Try walking for ten minutes a day, adding on as the weeks go by until you can walk for an hour. If you want to up your intensity level, try jogging or running. There are options available for every level of fitness. Many people focus on the reasons they can't exercise, not realizing that those are precisely the reasons why they need to commit to themselves.

Woman, equip yourself with the energy to pursue your dreams, and more energy will follow. If it comes down to the effort required to reach your goals and the frustration of failing to do so, the first is always worth whatever it costs. The undertaking of a dream that genuinely excites you will keep you motivated, naturally renewing your energy as you find yourself meeting milestones and drawing closer to your destiny. On the other hand, the stress of sitting back and letting opportunities pass you by will further rob you of energy and power. Stay motivated and draw on your inherent strength—enhanced by regular exercise—until you reach your dream.

THE PRICE OF OVERCOMING ANXIETY

An elevated heart rate, the sensation of tightness in the chest, sudden sweating, violent chills—most women will experience these telltale anxiety symptoms at some point in her life. My question for you is, do you ever feel this way, and, if so, can you identify any patterns that might help you recognize the circumstances and situations that might produce an onset of anxiety or even an attack? If you do, then you have an advantage. Many women encounter anxiety at unexpected moments and struggle to escape its effects.

Some elements that contribute to anxiety in women are female hormones and premenstrual symptoms. Although these factors don't affect all women equally, they seem to impact most of the female sex. I'm by no means suggesting that the mere fact of being a woman guarantees anxiety problems. As far as women's physiognomy and its effect on anxiety are concerned, many medical explanations remain elusive. But neither you nor I can wait for doctors to come up with an answer before we endeavor to manage the tension in our lives.

Indeed, it is universally understood that several effective ways of helping to relieve anxiety include adequate rest, proper nutrition, and exercise—these should sound familiar! But what many women don't understand is that anxiety is a mental health condition. I'm not calling anybody crazy; it's perfectly normal to feel anxiety at certain times. However, excessive anxiety—the unreasonable, ongoing worry that's hard to control and starts interfering with your daily activities—may be a disorder that goes beyond a natural reaction to a particular situation.

Anxiety stems from our brains, not our circumstances. Our minds make us who we are, and science hasn't advanced enough for us to be sure about all the ins and outs of how our brains work. In other words, science doesn't have all the answers we seek for managing our stress levels and regulating our moods. It doesn't have all the answers for the elements that govern our minds and thoughts. Thus, we need to seek a solution that is not only science based but also spiritual.

Anxiety hinders our ability to develop and exercise the most important virtues that all human beings must develop to have the best possible quality of life: the virtue of patience. Please don't confuse patience with passivity or inertia. The Bible says, *"Patience is better than power, and controlling one's emotions, than capturing a city"* (Proverbs 16:32 csb). In practicing patience, we exceed the value of wielding power, but we can't be patient when we're feeling anxious.

Your dreams require patience. Every woman who wants her dreams to come true must learn to wait. If there's an endeavor that teaches women to wait, it's motherhood—conceiving and waiting nine months to cradle your baby in your arms. No matter how much we long to meet our little one, we would not hasten the birth, or dire consequences might ensue. And so we wait, praying for patience, until an image on an ultrasound screen becomes a living, breathing being.

Anxiety causes many women to abandon their dreams. For other women, waiting patiently seems the opposite of working toward their goals. Suddenly the pressure is too much. It doesn't mean they're giving up, but they're not starting to shut the door to anxiety. Science may not have all the answers, but we don't have to sit around wondering if there's a cure for our anxiety. Thank God that we have resources beyond the natural to put an end to our worries! That's why we can't put the remedy for concern in the resources we have in the natural world alone. We have to turn to the spiritual elements.

With God, all things are possible. (See, for example, Matthew 19:26.) There is nothing that God cannot do. He may do things differently than you would have planned, and He can do them later than you would have preferred. Still, His ways and His timing are always better than anything you can imagine. Whether God goes ahead and reveals to you His plan for your life, or whether you find yourself waiting on Him and wondering what the plan is, the important thing is to know that with patience, by God's hand, you will achieve all your dreams.

I want to share with you two antidotes for anxiety. These tools are also helpful for improving our patience. One tool is spiritual, and the other one is natural.

SPIRITUAL TOOL: PRAYER

Prayer is such a powerful tool. Take a moment to say to God: "Lord, I'm open to whatever You have for me. It may not be what I planned, and it may not happen on my timetable, but I trust Your perfect plan for my life. I refuse to give up on You, but I choose to give up on worry, anxiety, and fear. I know nothing is too hard or too wonderful for You!"[36]

Today, decide to start doing whatever God is leading you to do. You may not have all the answers, and you may not know every step you'll need to take, but just take the first step by faith. Maybe that first step is to enroll in a local college class, forgive someone who hurt you, submit a resume for a job posting, or sign up for marriage counseling.

Ever since I started a relationship with the Lord, I have done two things continuously: serve in the church and pray. When I was a child, my parents would take my brothers, sisters, and me to the church to pray at five in the morning. To this day, one of my regular habits is rising at four in the morning to pray. You might be thinking, "Pastor, if I have to get up at four in the morning to pray, my anxiety will not decrease. It will increase!"

Praying early in the morning is not a requirement for Christians. That time of day simply works best for me for several reasons. First, I am used to getting up at that time to pray, as I have done so since I was a child. Second, my house is silent at that hour, giving me space and freedom to spend time in God's presence.

No matter what time of day you do it, prayer is one of the essential tools that God has given us to interact with Him and further His purposes for our lives. Prayer can bring clarity to our thoughts and can even propel our dreams to new heights. Have you ever seen things more clearly after talking matters over with a trusted friend or family member? If talking things through with other humans can help organize our thoughts and clarify our intentions, just think how much more a discussion with the omniscient Creator can aid us in thinking, analyzing,

---

36. Meyer, *You Can Begin Again*, 38.

and decision-making! Even so, your times of prayer should be simple, not complicated—just intimate conversations with your heavenly Father.

PRAYER CAN BRING CLARITY TO OUR THOUGHTS AND CAN EVEN PROPEL OUR DREAMS TO NEW HEIGHTS.

I always experience improved clarity and direction when I pray. My days—full of tasks, meetings, trips, counseling sessions, and more—flow more smoothly and with less anxiety because of my prayers. In my prayer time, I pray for my family, and then I present my whole day to God. I talk to Him about everything I'm going to do. Someone else looking on might make the same assumption that Eli the priest made about Hannah as she prayed with intensity in the temple—that she had consumed a little too much wine. (See 1 Samuel 1:9–18.) I'll admit that I talk to God with great emotion in my prayer time and while gesticulating dramatically, as we Latinas are apt to do. And as I do so, I feel a peace that my affairs, my day, my life, and my family are in the hands of the right Person.

Anxiety is overcome with prayer because my prayer is not designed to impress anyone with its eloquence. I have read the book of Psalms many times, and I am always impressed by David and the other authors' poetic beauty and skillful rhetoric as they express the collective and personal triumphs and nightmares they lived through. But such eloquence is not required of you and me. As long as we show reverence to God, we can express ourselves in our unique way. Jesus gave us these instructions for prayer:

When you pray, you shall not be like the hypocrites. For they love to pray standing in the synagogues and on the corners of the streets, that they may be seen by men. Assuredly, I say to you, they have their reward. But you, when you pray, go into your room, and when you have shut your door, pray to your Father who is in the secret place; and your Father who sees in secret will reward you openly. And when you pray, do not use vain repetitions as the heathen do. For they think that they will be heard for their many words.

(Matthew 6:5–7)

Just as the psalmists pour out their hearts and often record a direct experience of the Lord's help and presence, you, too, will often sense God's intervention during your prayer time. You will have the peace, security, and calm that your heart longs for, and you will be able to say, with the psalmist, "*Certainly God has heard me; He has attended to the voice of my prayer. Blessed be God, who has not turned away from my prayer, nor His mercy from me!*" (Psalm 66:19–20).

If it helps you be faithful in prayer, select a consistent time and place for your conversations with God. Some people pray or go to church only when problems are suffocating them. The best way is always to gather at church and pray. Believe me when I tell you that the level of anxiety in your life will drop significantly. When you develop the discipline of praying daily, you'll be able to attest to the truth of what I'm telling you. For me, beginning every day in prayer is the best way; it's starting on the right foot.

People often mistake me and think that I pray only first thing in the morning, never at any other time of day. On the contrary, I make a habit of following Paul's injunction to "*pray without ceasing*" (1 Thessalonians 5:17). I pray all the time! In some cases, a specific event will prompt me to break away from whatever I'm doing and present that issue to God in prayer. Prayer is, among other things, that spiritual place where you can release your pressures and affirm your belief that God keeps you close. He also gives you rest, revives you, and redirects you on the right path.

I believe with all my heart that regular prayer, and even our mere faith in God, is a better remedy than any physical medicine for the mental illness of anxiety. Prayer provides a time of healing for your soul and your thoughts and a key to finding the power to pursue your dreams.

NATURAL TOOL: PLANNING

Anxiety can seem like an automatic response to things outside our control. And when we don't have control over the things we think we ought to control, our stress usually increases, sometimes astronomically. That's why I believe there is no more significant cause of anxiety than a chaotic life. There will always be external events that you cannot control. To maintain our balance when those uncontrollable, external elements show up in our lives, we need to have our day-to-day existence as orderly and optimally organized as possible.

I think there are three things you should always keep in order in your life: your environment, your time, and your energy. Our environment is the area that surrounds us. I can't comprehend how anyone can live with stuff scattered all around them. For me to experience peace, I need to have my environment tidy and well-organized. I've heard some people complain that having to clean their homes and tidy up their space takes away their peace, and I don't understand them. How can you lead a peaceful existence when you constantly have to search for the items you need because you don't have an organized home? A messy house makes for a messy life. It's as simple as that.

Start by assigning a specific place for each of the items you use daily, such as your phone, keys, eyeglasses, wallet, and so forth. Believe me, your life will start to flow more easily. If you've had to fight with the clothes in your closet, if you spend more than a minute searching for the pair of shoes you want to wear, if you have ten purses and can't use any of them because they're all full of papers and junk—your life can't possibly be peaceful. But if you'll set aside a day to organize your closet so that you can see everything; if you'll keep a purse insert of essential items that you can transfer from one bag to another—these changes and others, though small, can make a big difference in making your environment more organized and your life more orderly.

Once you've organized your closet and your purses, you can move on to other parts of your house, your office, and even your car. When your environment is working for you and making your life easier, your anxiety level is sure to drop significantly. Having your surroundings in optimal condition will help your whole life flow more easily. Once you've planned out the organization of those surroundings, you reduce the stress of searching for things and trying to remember where you put them. An organized purse, for example, contains only what you need without being weighed down by so many items that you can't even wade through its contents. The same goes for your drawers, closets, and car—all the elements of your environment. Align everything around you with a plan that complements your schedule, your habits, and your tastes. There is ample need for improvisation daily; any area you can plan and be prepared for will help you solve problems while experiencing minimal stress and anxiety.

Another example of an area where planning proves helpful is the food we eat. If we plan out our menus for the coming week, we won't need to be anxious about what we are going to eat or what we will cook. Can you imagine how much time we would waste if, every time we were hungry, we went to the pantry and stood there trying to figure out what to make? To me, planning menus and shopping for groceries accordingly is a far more organized method of keeping my family fed. Maybe you come up with a pattern of cooking soup on Monday, pasta on Tuesday, salad on Wednesday, meat on Thursday, and so on. When you do your grocery shopping, you know what you need to buy, and you don't have to spend an extra minute of your time thinking about what you're going to cook or eat that day.

Now, if you find that on the day you usually cook pasta, you feel like having a hamburger, and it's convenient enough to change up the menu, go ahead and cook a hamburger. But by keeping up a pattern, you can save yourself a significant amount of time and effort.

I like to organize the other aspects of my life in the same way that I plan out our weekly meals. After my morning prayer time, the next thing I do is plan my day, mentally reviewing all the things I need to do and when. I repeat that routine in the car every morning while driving my daughters Jenibelle and Jillianne to school. We start by praying together, and then my daughters always say, "Today's plans." Right there, we talk about everything that everyone has to do when they get home from school. They begin their day in prayer and planning, too.

In the short-term and the long-term, your time should be planned out as much as it can be. You may be asking, "Do I have to plan absolutely *everything?*" There will be unforeseen circumstances and factors beyond your control. Yet I recommend making a plan for everything you can so that the elements you cannot control will have space to fit into your daily routine. I like to anticipate how I will spend the hours of my day, the days of my week, the weeks of my month, the months of my year, and the years of my decades. Planning reduces anxiety because you know how you plan to spend the next moment that you have to live, whether it's in the next hour or the next decade. The improvised life can feel more relaxed in the moment, but later on, when you look back and realize how much time was lost, you may face glaring regrets.

The third thing you should plan out to decrease your anxiety is your energy. You've probably heard of people planning their environments and organizing their time, but did it ever occur to you that we can plan how we'll expend our energy on a given day? I'm talking about anticipating what you will focus on and devote your attention to every day. Woman, you need to plan your focus! And if something is not within the scope of that predetermined focus—barring urgent situations and emergencies, of course—do not spend a minute of your time or attention on it. If you've planned to focus on your family, stop looking at other people's families; look after your own.

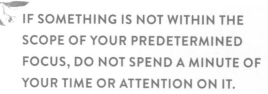

IF SOMETHING IS NOT WITHIN THE SCOPE OF YOUR PREDETERMINED FOCUS, DO NOT SPEND A MINUTE OF YOUR TIME OR ATTENTION ON IT.

Women are naturally gifted at multitasking, so it's easy for us to take on more tasks than we ought to—and to suffer as a result. For example, rather than doing our job to the best of our abilities, we may do just enough on the job because we're busy checking up on other people or measuring ourselves against their progress. Trying to pay attention to too many topics can cause real anxiety. Focus on your own family, business, priorities, plans, and dreams, and let everyone else focus on theirs. I have assisted hundreds of women who've told me various versions of the same story: "Look, Pastor, I've been very effective at doing such and such, but this other person...she's making these mistakes, and she doesn't even realize it." My response to such reports is always the same question: "How does it affect you?" In most cases, the issue does not directly affect the person who is telling me about it. Stop wasting your energy worrying about what others are doing, and just focus on doing your personal best.

Always check your intentions when you feel compelled to correct someone else or offer advice. If someone asks for help, give it gladly, but don't expend your precious time and energy on faultfinding and correcting. I'm thinking in particular of all the women who have put their lives and dreams on hold by worrying over and suffering for their children who no longer live under their roof. Once your children have chosen their course and don't need your day-to-day assistance any longer, you need to let go of any efforts to control them and simply entrust their steps to the Lord.

It is unfortunate how many women focus their energy on the wrong places. Narrow your focus on issues that have to do with your dreams and pertain to what God has called you to do, and stop spending your efforts on trying to correct and direct the lives of others. Goodness knows you'll need all the energy and wisdom available to you to pursue your dreams! In the next and final chapter, I'll share some strategies for maximizing that energy and wisdom.

Surround yourself

with dreamers who

inspire and encourage

you to dream.

DISCIPLINED TO DREAM

*M*any people consider motivation to be the essential key to achieving a dream. While I recognize that motivation can inspire us and energize us, it seems to me that motivation has its limits. What do we do when we tire of waiting for our dream to come true? If our motivation fades and we've lost our inspiration, what happens? That's the potential problem with motivation. It may be present today and act as the fuel that gets me going, but it can also disappear in the blink of an eye. It is in such moments when we can't depend on motivation that we must turn to personal discipline. While a sudden lack of motivation threatens to knock you down and keep you from moving forward, discipline will keep you steady and help you stay on your feet. Discipline is a powerful attribute that is essential to the pursuit and fulfillment of all our dreams. Without discipline, you are unlikely to push past the occasional losses of inspiration and lags in motivation that are likely to come.

Just what is discipline? Simply put, discipline is doing what we must do when we must do it, without overthinking the situation or coming up with excuses. Discipline allows us to plan out, decide on, and execute our actions, desires, and feelings without interruption.

The word *discipline* is often associated with punishment. You may have grown up in a household where your parents enacted harsh "discipline," giving the term a negative connotation in your mind. But discipline need not involve painful consequences or brutal repression. Quite the opposite! When practiced in a positive sense, discipline keeps us on track to meet our goals and achieve our dreams.

The first dictionary entry under the term *discipline* offers this definition: "orderly or prescribed conduct or pattern of behavior; self-control." When we apply an orderly approach to the pursuit of our dreams, we can accomplish more than we ever imagined. There are few sources of personal satisfaction greater than achieving that which you set out to do, and personal discipline is a significant key to meeting those accomplishments. Even if your parents were strict in their "discipline" of you as a child, that term need not bring you sadness and anguish any longer. Let it become a word that connotes joy, comfort, and happiness as you take a disciplined approach to pursue your dreams.

THE BENEFITS OF DISCIPLINE

A structured, disciplined lifestyle propels you to execute your goals even when you don't feel like it. Discipline helps you take small actions, every day, in all areas of your life, with the higher intention of gradually achieving your goals. For example, if you want to become an avid reader, discipline yourself by setting aside a certain amount of time every day to read and gradually increase the duration of your reading time over a few days or weeks. Before you know it, you will have polished off more books than you ever imagined you could.

On days when your motivation lags, you may feel discouraged and fatigued; you may be tempted to leave your books on the shelf. But discipline will say to you, "No matter how you feel, today and every day, you must open a book and execute your goal." With discipline, you can silence those voices of self-sabotage that have kept you from pursuing other dreams. Ask any highly successful person about the secret to success, and he or she will probably mention discipline. This attribute is vital in all areas of your life, from personal relationships to spiritual growth to career pursuits.

Discipline empowers you to practice self-control rather than being controlled by other people or your circumstances. It also gives you the self-confidence you need to solve any challenge that comes your way. A disciplined woman feels capable and confident that she can, and will, achieve her goals and objectives.

A life of discipline is also a life of focus. When you are disciplined, you know perfectly well what you are aiming for and the reasons why, and your thoughts, words, and actions all align with your dreams. By being disciplined, you guard against distractions and become less likely to rely on excuses.

Finally, a life of discipline brings satisfaction. Discipline helps you achieve success and feel the well-being and pleasure you crave. Every time you act on your goals, you feel satisfied that you have made it. No matter how small a step you may take, you will reap the reward of satisfaction. Discipline should be a habit of life that governs our actions to help us go our way toward the realization of our dreams.

THE POWER OF HABITS

Discipline transforms into the development of conscious habits. You can develop a lifestyle that is consistent with all your dreams through your practices. Good eating habits are consistent with a healthy life. A sedentary lifestyle is not compatible with an active life. When you know your dreams, through discipline, you can achieve those habits that are congruent with what you're seeking, and there is no way you can't make it.

Discipline seals habits in you. If your mind asks you to give up in any area, your discipline will put your mind to work no matter what negative message it carries. Your thoughts will no longer be able to take you away from your goals. A disciplined mind will recognize all the reasons you should do what you want to do, regardless of how you feel. This way, little by little, your mind will develop more and more control and self-discipline, and you will be closer to achieving your dreams.

Designing good habits helps you achieve your goals or objectives. You will never again be a victim of those voices that sabotage your progress. With or without motivation, good habits drive you to action, to movement. Good habits eradicate the inertia in your life where days, weeks, months, and years go by, and nothing good happens. Your actions will align with your goals and dreams. You will be in control of your life and closer to the results you desire.

I am determined to share with other women what I know and what works for me to live to the fullest and realize my dreams. The following are just some of the habits I have found essential to pursuing my dreams.

DEVELOPING HEALTHY HABITS

Pay close attention to your activities throughout the day, and you may be surprised by the number of tasks you perform out of habit. Many of us may think that we are acting on our own volition in ways that mold our environment. Still, the reality is often that we are being shaped by our environment—that we are acting out of habit rather than being intentional about what we do. We need to make sure that our environments give us ample space and flexibility for pursuing our dreams. In the words of Touré Roberts, "In order to fulfill your purpose in life, you have to dwell in environments that unlock your potential and releases [sic] the creativity that God has placed inside of you."[37]

In psychological terms, a "habit" is a behavior that we repeat, whether consciously or unconsciously, which is already a part of our life. For us to turn a desired behavior into a habit, we need to practice it over and over again. According to a study published in 2009, it takes more than two months—just about 66 days, in fact—for a new habit to form; this time "can vary widely depending on the behavior, the person, and the circumstances."[38] Behavior does not become habitual because of a mental decision alone. We must practice the desired behavior repeatedly until it has become a part of our routine.

Good habits are those that make positive growth possible. They allow us to improve, mature, set worthy goals, and achieve our objectives. On the other hand, bad habits limit our development, prevent us from becoming better, and stifle our true

---

37. Touré Roberts, *Purpose Awakening: Discover the Epic Idea That Motivated Your Birth* (New York: FaithWords, 2014), 31.
38. James Clear, "How Long Does it Actually Take to Form a New Habit? (Backed by Science)," JamesClear.com, accessed May 10, 2021, https://jamesclear.com/new-habit.

selves. How do we develop bad habits? Many of our poor habits stem from unhealthy relationships, whether with other people or with certain substances. Some bad habits include substance abuse, procrastination, lying, and cheating—all toxic habits stemming from toxic relationships. How do we eliminate the unhealthy habits we may have been practicing?

STEPS TO ELIMINATING UNHEALTHY HABITS

1. Don't associate with the wrong people. *"Do not be deceived: 'Evil company corrupts good habits'"* (1 Corinthians 15:33).

2. Be yourself—and be comfortable with who you are. Some women admire and idealize others to the point of desiring to be them and not themselves. Trying to be someone you're not is hard, exhausting work, and the attempt will keep you living in fear of being discovered. Your most rewarding relationships will be with the people who know the real you and appreciate you for who you are, not for who they want you to be.

3. Don't lie to yourself. Realize that not everything is terrible, and not everything is okay. Don't be afraid to acknowledge how you're feeling. Honesty is always the best policy, especially when it comes to being honest with yourself. When you deceive yourself, you will know it deep down. It's best to be honest with the most crucial person in your life: yourself.

4. Accept the fact that you can and will make mistakes. In the words of Alexander Pope, "To err is human, to forgive divine." None of us is perfect. The only way to avoid making mistakes is to do absolutely nothing, and those who are afraid to mess up will lead miserable

existences of paralysis and inertia. The more things you avoid because of fear of failure, the more regrets you end up having. Perfectionists tend to be some of the most frustrated and least fulfilled people in the world.

5. Don't wait until you're "ready." Some people don't start anything because they're always missing something. Life will always find a way to surprise you. Opportunities arise when you least expect them. You can never be ready, but don't let this stop you. When an opportunity comes into your life unexpectedly, take it if you feel so led. When you have to do something, please do it. Don't just stand there waiting for a later date.

6. Realize that complaining and wallowing in self-pity will get you nowhere. Who of us ever solved a problem by dwelling on it and feeling sorry for ourselves? Focus on finding the good, positive aspects of every situation, and you will start to realize that your most significant difficulties are often only a matter of perspective.

THE CYCLE OF HABIT FORMATION

When you understand the cycle of habit formation, you can use it to create good, desirable habits to help eradicate bad habits.

1. **Signal:** That which activates your behavior or habit reminds you that it is time to make a habit of it. Examples: a schedule, a season, an alarm.

2. **Routine:** The habit itself and the steps behind it.

3. **Reward:** What you get in return for observing the habit; a prize, of sorts, whether actual or experienced in the mind. Many good habits have implicit rewards, but you can reward yourself throughout the day as you achieve small victories, thereby increasing the likelihood of your continuing the excellent habit from now on.

To develop a new habit, be sure to make a plan for how you will adopt it, what you will do when things get complicated, or how obstacles get in the way.

CURATE YOUR CIRCLE OF DREAMERS

One of the best ways to improve a skill is to practice it with someone better at it than you. If you want to get better at playing tennis, you might practice with a professional. If you're going to become a better writer, you might enlist a published author as your mentor. If you want to improve your cooking skills, you might take classes from a recognized chef. To hone your musical talents, you might take lessons with a concert pianist or a professional vocalist. Yes, you will have to work harder, think faster, and learn more fundamentals to match someone whose caliber is so far above yours. This idea of playing with someone better than you translates very well into your personal and professional success. That's why it's essential to surround yourself with winners.

SURROUND YOURSELF WITH PEOPLE WHO CHALLENGE YOU

Many entrepreneurs aspire to be the most intelligent person in the room on every subject. But if you're always the most intelligent person, you're limiting yourself. This mentality leads us to surround ourselves with people who will not propel us into our future but will only slow our progress as they depend on us for help.

On one occasion, a real estate agent told a family member who was buying a house in a privileged location that if they bought the smallest house, they would reap the highest profit. The other properties and homes, more luxurious and with larger footprints, would increase the value of that property. I thought to myself, "If I lived in a smaller house, I would feel disadvantaged." But the real estate agent was right. The value of the other properties increased that of the smaller property.

Many women choose friendships only with those who don't put any pressure on them. They prefer to surround themselves with people they feel superior to, if only slightly, perhaps in career success or personal appearance. Some of us want to be the smartest in the group or possess the most valuable property. But that kind of thinking keeps us stuck in our comfort zone, where we are apt to settle down and stay complacent rather than seeking and striving to do our best.

Life is full of challenges. We won't win every time; there will always be obstacles and detractors along our path to success. During those moments, nothing feels better than having someone to share your fears and doubts: friends and mentors who listen to you and encourage you to be the best you can. In dark moments, for many people, looking upward means only seeing God. It has often been God leading me to other people who, despite challenges and adverse circumstances, have overcome and gone on to achieve their dreams. Whether we realize it's happening or not, we become like the people with whom we spend the most time. We behave like them, think like them, look like them, and even decide based on what we think those people would do.

For example, many research findings show that we are more likely to gain weight if a close friend or family member is overweight.[39] Similarly, we are more likely to participate in an exercise program if we surround ourselves with fit, health-oriented people.

> WHETHER WE REALIZE IT'S HAPPENING OR NOT, WE BECOME LIKE THE PEOPLE WITH WHOM WE SPEND THE MOST TIME.

I love people who challenge me. I love people who have already achieved what I aspire to do. I love being in circles where I know I have a lot to learn. When we meet those who challenge us, we may tend to push them away, sometimes in frustration or with a sense that we will never be as good as they are. What we need to do is to be motivated. When I meet someone who has reached a place I want to be or achieved a dream of mine, I don't feel frustrated; I feel challenged, and that feeling motivates me, inspires me, and moves me.

CULTIVATE A SUPPORT SYSTEM

It's time to rethink how we use our social networks. Most social networking sites serve only as a confirmation of what we can't do, haven't done, or don't think we can achieve. If you were to see everything that happens behind every seemingly perfect scene, you would realize that, in most cases, a lot of work and

---

39. Christine Junge, "How your friends make you fat—the social network of weight," *Harvard Health Blog*, May 24, 2011, https://www.health. harvard.edu/blog/how-your-friends-make-you-fat—the-social-network-of-weight-201105242666.

effort went into creating what appears to have been a spontaneous snapshot.

It's time to focus on your real-life relationships—not your virtual ones—and analyze each one of them. Maybe you need to rethink the people you spend time with and allow to influence you. Analyze your circles. Do they make you feel and think positively? Do they inspire and motivate you to be the best version of yourself? Do they support and encourage you to achieve your goals? Do they challenge you? Or do they tell you, "You can't do it," "It's not possible," "You're not good enough," "You're bound to fail"? Find and focus on relationships with those who can celebrate your successes and accomplishments. We waste our lives if we surround ourselves with people who do not invite us to do or be our best.

Don't tolerate anyone around you who makes you feel less than or tells you that you can't achieve what you set out to do. If anyone in your life makes you feel emotionally drained, it's time to phase out that relationship and make room for those who will contribute to your future and share your faith in your dreams. Detoxify your life by getting rid of any relationships that are not working positively for you.

Surround yourself with a circle of dreamers. Look for women who are just as motivated as you are to achieve their dreams. You will motivate them, and they will motivate you because motivation and inspiration are contagious.

Your relationships and your closest circles are an essential key to walking in the pursuit of your dreams and God's desires for you. Have the courage to eliminate negative people from your life and watch your strength become renewed. Your enthusiasm automatically flourishes with it. Leaving relationships that don't work for you is critical if you want to achieve your dreams.

I have many friends. Some of them challenge me too much. There are some whom I have to push and motivate regularly. In both circles, I know my place. Glory to God for those you have to drive and push! Blessed be God when He allows us to move someone to be a better person. But never forget that you need those who are going to put pressure on you to move. We all need people to push us out of our comfort zone and put us in front of our dreams to run for them until we reach them.

Conclusion

THE TIME TO ACT IS NOW!

Thousands of women dream. Some women dream of small goals because they don't think they can aspire for more. Other women dare to dream big. However, both groups often postpone fulfilling their dreams with excuses that, if looked at closely, reflect their insecurities. Are they worthy of getting where they want? Would God want something so great for them? Are they not dreaming of "the impossible"? And so the dream remains a dream, never becoming a reality.

However, God won't give you a dream without also providing you the ability to make it come true. Your dreams are God's dreams for you. It would help if you took it upon yourself to write a plan of action (remember Habakkuk 2:2–4?) and do your part—that which is within reach today. What seems impossible is God's job. He is the One who gives you favor in the eyes of others and every situation. He is the One who opens the right doors, those you can't unlock by your efforts. He is the One who puts the right words in your mouth when you need them. He is the One who brings the right people into your life.

You are responsible for seeing what God places before you, beyond your natural eyes, aligning it with your vision, and moving to see your dreams come true. And you are called to be steadfast in the face of adversity and to keep believing in your dream. In the moments when doubt steals your hope because you encounter obstacles while working toward your vision, remember that the One who gave you the promise will fulfill it.

Believe in your dream and act on it, regardless of what your circumstances seem to say or what other people say against it. The bigger your dream, the more confident you can be that it came from God because we serve a God of big dreams. And when your dream comes true, don't "fall asleep" because you did it. It is up to you to keep it alive, administer it, extend its blessing, and enlarge it without limit because God's dreams are dreams with a purpose for you and all those within your reach.

There are so many beautiful elements in your character, woman, that cannot die with you. Just as there are people who have marked your life in a special and unexpected way, you have the ability—and the responsibility—to make a positive mark in the lives of others. Each of the dreams you will give birth to, each experience that helps you grow, and each act of self-improvement will be the instrument that God uses to inspire other people to face their challenges and achieve success in every area of their lives.

Being able to inspire isn't just a characteristic of a woman who values herself. Inspiring is a life assignment driven by your ability to live to the fullest, with the right attitude and a steadfast focus. Inspiring is a demonstration of love for those around you whom your life experience allows you to touch. Sometimes, we want to turn the page on our own life because we desire to move toward new horizons and birth new beginnings. However, that page doesn't have to remain in a closed book. Each one of the pages of our life must and can be read by those women who are going through the experiences we have already successfully overcome.

JUST AS THERE ARE PEOPLE WHO HAVE MARKED YOUR LIFE IN A SPECIAL AND UNEXPECTED WAY, YOU HAVE THE ABILITY AND THE RESPONSIBILITY TO MAKE A POSITIVE MARK IN THE LIVES OF OTHERS.

Your dreams, your ingenuity, and the inspiration you can be for others—all this shines forth for all to see when you value yourself and faithfully follow the One who gave you a vision for the future. Please don't delay your dream any longer but seize it today!

ABOUT THE AUTHOR

𝒪mayra Font is a fulfilled woman who has fought for her dreams. She continues to dream big, not only for herself but for her marriage, her daughters, her ministry, and the women she preaches to and supports.

She knows what it is like to face and overcome adversity and stand firm in the Lord. A successful businesswoman with a steady pace and financial wisdom, she has balanced being a supportive and encouraging wife, a loving and dedicated mother, and a woman of God whose priority is her pastoral ministry.

Her messages are heard in Pura Palabra Media's radio station in Puerto Rico, Orlando, Florida, and online through pura-palabra.com.

She and her husband, Otoniel, have four daughters: Joanirie, Janaimar, Jenibelle, and Jillianne. Pastoring Fuente de Agua Viva churches in Puerto Rico and Orlando, Florida, and as founder and director of Fountain Christian Bilingual School, she lives in Puerto Rico with her family.

Welcome to Our House!

We Have a Special Gift for You

It is our privilege and pleasure to share in your love of Christian books. We are committed to bringing you authors and books that feed, challenge, and enrich your faith.

To show our appreciation, we invite you to sign up to receive a specially selected **Reader Appreciation Gift**, with our compliments. Just go to the Web address at the bottom of this page.

God bless you as you seek a deeper walk with Him!

WE HAVE A GIFT FOR YOU. VISIT:

whpub.me/nonfictionthx

WHITAKER
HOUSE